"Kimberlee Conway Ireton's writ   a deep prayer life and joyful obec   as she describes her emotions: an   contentment and longing for mo   an intimate look into a year of he...   draw near to God with her."

~**Lynne M. Baab**, author of *Joy Together* and *Sabbath Keeping*

"If you want to read a beautifully written, often painfully honest account of trying to pay attention to God through the rigors of mother-hood, start here. Kimberlee holds nothing back—joy, depression, fatigue, faith crises, and holy moments. In the end, it feels less like a book about parenting children and more about God's parenting of us. It will help you pay attention to your life."

~**Dan Baumgartner**, Senior Pastor, First Presbyterian Church of Hollywood

"A fearlessly honest memoir. Bravely sharing the dark places of her spir-itual struggles, Kimberlee Conway Ireton recounts her journey through postpartum depression with a balance of humor and humility. This memoir resonates long after the last words have been read. I laughed and cried, and found a kindred soul within these pages."

~**Kris Camealy**, author of *Holey, Wholly, Holy*

"Kimberlee Conway Ireton writes a boldly honest story that reads like a confession. Her book is a persistent digging to find the light…a story of God's enduring faithfulness, and it is a revelation of the Father's love for her, and for all of us."

~**Jennifer Dukes Lee**, author of *Love Idol*

Cracking Up

a postpartum faith crisis

Kimberlee Conway Ireton

ML

Mason Lewis
Press

Mason Lewis Press
Seattle
http://masonlewispress.com

Cover photo by Mark Wragg, iStockphoto®
Cover design by Sprague Minger, sprague@spragueminger.com

Printed in the United States of America

Library of Congress Cataloging-in-Publication Data:

Conway Ireton, Kimberlee, 1975-

      Cracking Up: A Postpartum Faith Crisis / Kimberlee Conway Ireton

          p. cm.

      Includes bibliographical references (p. 256).

      ISBN: 978-0-9896725-0-4 (paperback)

      LCCN: 2013913027

For Jack, Jane, Luke, and Ben,
        who bring me daily joy
and for Doug,
        who keeps me laughing

contents

a word about the church year

The church year is the lens through which I see my life, and since two of the central events in this story occurred on Good Friday and Epiphany, it only made sense to structure the book accordingly. For those unfamiliar with the liturgical calendar, here is a brief overview.

The church year begins in Advent, a four-week season of preparation for Christmas, which is a 12-day season of celebrating Christ's birth. After Christmas is the season of Epiphany, which begins on January 6, the day we celebrate the coming of the Magi to the Christ Child.

Epiphany fades into Lent on Ash Wednesday. Lent is a season of repentance and fasting to prepare us for Easter. The final three days of Lent are known as the Triduum (pronounced *trid*-ee-um), when we remember the last three days of Jesus' earthly life: Maundy Thursday, when He instituted the Last Supper and was arrested; Good Friday, when He was crucified, died, and was buried; and Holy Saturday, when His body lay in the earth.

Then, of course, comes Easter, the second-longest season of the church year, in which we celebrate Jesus' resurrection.

Only Ordinary Time is longer, stretching from the feast of Pentecost at the end of the Easter season to the beginning of Advent (and a new church year) in late November or early December.

Advent
the baby cometh
(december)

Too eager I must not be to understand.
How should the work the Master goes about
Fit the vague sketch my compasses have planned?
I am his house—for him to go in and out.
He builds me now—and if I cannot see
At any time what he is doing with me,
'Tis that he makes the house for me too grand.

—George MacDonald, *Diary of an Old Soul*

good times

The year began so auspiciously. My first book had come out the previous November—a lifelong dream come true—and I was still riding the giddy wave of being a Published Author.

Then I got my first quarter sales report. In three months, 800 copies of my book had sold. I stared at that number, trying to make an extra zero appear at the end of it.

My visions of hefty royalty payments evaporated. I emailed my writer friend Lynne and asked her if this was normal. She emailed back and said 800 wasn't great, but it was better than her first book had done in the first quarter. I felt mildly better.

Then I got my second quarter sales report. In the second three months of publication, my book had sold only 400 additional copies.

My hope of any royalty payments evaporated.

Around this same time, a family friend had a baby. My husband held the new little guy after church one Sunday. When we got home, he started to make squawking sounds about wanting another baby.

"Absolutely not," I said as I folded the pile of clothes on our bed. I held up a pair of our daughter's toddler-sized pajamas. "This is the age I like them. When they're old enough to tell you what's wrong and to pee in the toilet." I folded the jammies and laid them on the bed. "We're done having babies."

"But they're so cute," Doug said, and the way he said "cute" made me realize he was more than half serious.

I gave him my most scornful are-you-flipping-kidding-me look.

"They cry all the time and don't let you sleep."

"Just think about it." He folded another pair of Jane's pj's and added it to the pile.

"I don't have to think about it. We said we'd have two kids. We have two kids. We're done. Besides," I added, as if this settled the matter, "we gave away all our baby stuff after Jane was born."

But Doug continued to mention this third baby. I chalked it up to the fact that he would be turning 40 in December and wanting a baby was his way of dealing with midlife, his version of a Porsche. Alas, I am not strong-willed. I am a people-pleaser. I want people, especially people I love, to be happy. So as Doug continued to make baby comments through summer and into fall, I began to waver.

"Maybe it wouldn't be so bad," I told myself. "Maybe it would be fun."

"Fun?" I answered myself. "Fun? What are you smoking?"

I wasn't smoking. I was feeling the horrible thud that comes after riding giddy wings of anticipation. When my book was published at the end of last year, I'd envisioned my career as a writer unfolding before me in brick upon brick of gold, paving my way straight to the Emerald City of multi-published authordom. Unfortunately, it seemed that the powers that be in the publishing world hadn't gotten the Emerald City memo. I'd been trying all year to publish articles in magazines—sending query letters when appropriate and actually writing the article and sending it with a cover letter if necessary (and it was often necessary; Doug says this is what puts the "free" in freelancing). I was hoping to get a byline or two this way, and maybe earn a little extra money, since I sure wasn't going to earn anything from my book. But most of these queries came back with a polite rejection letter. Even the pre-written articles came back with a thanks-but-no-thanks.

That wasn't the worst of it, though. I hadn't poured my heart and soul into those articles. The project on which I was focusing most of my time and attention and on which I was lavishing all my authorial love was my young adult novel. Over the past six years, I'd written it and rewritten it—and rewritten it again. Six years felt like a long gestation, and I was ready to push it out into the world. So in April I began trying to find an agent for my baby. All but one of my 20 queries came back with rejection emails. Okay, that's not exactly true. Half of them had if-you-don't-hear-back-in-a-month-I'm-not-interested policies with a please-don't-follow-up-if-you-don't-hear-from-me addendum to prevent needy writer-types like me from pestering them about our queries. Needless to say, I didn't hear back in a month. Except from one. That one agent asked for a partial. I gladly—euphorically!—sent her the first 50 pages of my manuscript and crossed my fingers and prayed, "Please oh please oh please let her want the rest."

In June, I sent my editor a proposal for a second non-fiction book, a book he suggested I write. He asked for some revisions and for a marketing plan. I sent revisions and a marketing plan. He passed on my proposal. Even though I cried, I was also relieved. My heart wasn't in this book. It was in my novel, my poor, rejected, unwanted novel.

By October, I had a stack of rejection letters nearly an inch thick. I also had my first year sales report in hand. If I'd thought things were bad before, they were much worse now. In June, July, and August, more people returned copies of my book than bought them. I had three months of *negative* sales. I didn't even know that was possible. I forgot about royalty payments and began to pray my publisher wouldn't decide to pull my book off the shelves and out of print.

Through it all, Doug continued to hold every brand new baby at church and make wistful comments about how cute and sweet they were and wouldn't it be fun to have another one of our own?

And so, I wavered.

"Babies need you," I told myself. "Unlike editors and agents, who don't give a fig about you, you are the center of the baby's universe."

"Sure," I answered myself. "That's just what you want, to be a black hole of sleep-deprivation and milk production."

"Well," my wounded writer self retorted, "at least I'd be producing something somebody wanted."

Then, in early December, the agent—the one on whom hung all my writerly hopes—rejected the partial of my novel manuscript she'd had for three months. Though I'd been telling myself for those three months that she would probably reject it, psyching myself out like that doesn't really work because secretly I was hoping she'd fall in love with it and beg me to let her represent me. Like she'd even have to beg. It's not like there were any other contenders.

But she didn't want it.

And that's when I realized I couldn't possibly have another baby. Not if I was going to be a writer. Not if I was going to press on through all this rejection and come out on the other side with a second book to my name. Not if I was going to be able to parent the two kids I already had, write, and stay any sort of sane—because writing was what kept me sane. Words are how I see the world, how I make sense of it. Without words, there is no meaning, there is no *me*. At least, no me that I can make sense of or understand. Forming words into sentences and paragraphs and stories—this is the only way I know to truly live. Having another baby would just be one more giant responsibility sucking my time and energy away from my writing, away from the words that give me life. I knew Doug would be disappointed, and I hated disappointing him, but I also knew I was simply not emotionally, psychologically, or spiritually able to have another baby.

A week later, I found out I was pregnant.

"I warned you," said my friend Tiffany, who was six months pregnant with her own should-we-shouldn't-we third baby. "Ambivalence is yes."

Thus the year ended: I had a stack of rejection letters an inch thick, my book was tanking, there was no second book deal on or even over the horizon, no one wanted my beloved novel, and I was a weepy, hormonal, pregnant mess.

Good times. And baby, they were about to get better.

Triduum
the end of life as I know it
(april)

I heard this old man speak when I was pregnant, someone who had been sober for fifty years, a very prominent doctor. He said that he'd finally figured out a few years ago that his profound sense of control, in the world and over his life, is another addiction and a total illusion. He said that when he sees little kids sitting in the backseat of cars in those car seats that have steering wheels, with grim expressions of concentration on their faces, clearly convinced that their efforts are causing the car to do whatever it is doing, he thinks of himself and his relationship with God: God who drives along silently, gently amused, in the real driver's seat.

—Anne Lamott, *Operating Instructions*

Maundy Thursday
the cup of tears

It is the beginning of the end. The darkest three days of the liturgical year, the triduum, begin today. I do not know how the days could get much darker. These weeks of Lent have felt like darkness, darkness, darkness. Like the valley of the shadow.

Two months ago, shortly before Ash Wednesday, Elaine left me a voice mail asking me to call her back. I thought she was going to ask me to help her plan Tiffany's baby shower.

But when I called her, she said, "I have sad news."

My heart fell into my feet. I thought Tiffany must have lost her baby.

"About our sweet little Michaela." Michaela is Tiffany's second daughter, my Jane's best friend. "She has leukemia."

I blinked. I couldn't have heard right. "But—" I stammered, "—but we just had a play date with her and Madeline on Friday." Tiffany and I had commiserated about how miserable pregnancy was. She said she was so grateful she only had six more weeks till this baby was out of her body and she could stop feeling sick all the time.

I shook my head. "How—how can she have leukemia?" I couldn't believe it.

Elaine told me how Michaela had woken up Saturday with a horrible stomachache. Her dad had taken her to the doctor, who saw some swelling in her liver and sent her over to Children's Hospital. She'd been diagnosed that afternoon.

I felt stunned. How could this be happening? Leukemia? Michaela? She was fine two days ago. How could she have leukemia? It didn't make any sense.

Two weeks later, on Ash Wednesday, we went to church in the evening. When we came to the front of the sanctuary and our pastor, Jim, marked my forehead with a cross, and Doug's too, when he marked Jack's and Jane's little foreheads with crosses, when he said to each of us, "Remember that you are dust, and to dust you will return," it felt all too real. Too possible. Too scary. To know that my kids could die, that Doug could die, that I could die, with these children unraised and my novel unpublished. I could not swallow for the tears that choked my throat.

Now, six weeks later, it's Maundy Thursday, and I have lived Lent this year. When evening comes, we go to church. I sit in the third row from the pulpit, with Jack on one side of me and Jane on the other, Doug next to her. As the lights dim after each reading, each song, I think of the cancer growing in Michaela's bone marrow, of the pile of rejection letters growing in my desk drawer, of this baby growing in my belly. Mostly I think of how fragile and uncertain life is.

I feel afraid. And drained, as if my faith has fled and left me shriveled and dried out in the wilderness. In the dark.

And yeah, I know God is with me in the dark. I know He meets us in our brokenness and need. I went to seminary. I know all the right theological answers.

But in this dark season, I do not want a God who humbly meets me in brokenness. I want a God who exercises enemy-annihilating power, as Jim put it in a sermon a few weeks ago. I want God to obliterate the cancer that is eating Michaela's bone marrow. I want God to eradicate my pregnancy-induced queasiness—both the physical and the emotional kind. I want God to make an agent love my novel as much as I do, to make a publisher love it, and readers, too. I want God to show up with power and might, to raise His victorious right hand and for all to be well.

This is what I have wanted all these long dark weeks of Lent. It is what I want as I sit here in the third pew of our darkening sanctuary, a child on either side of me and one growing within me.

By the time Jim steps into the pulpit, most of the lights in the sanctuary have been extinguished, and I sit, literally, in darkness. Jim opens his meditation by mentioning that the word Maundy comes from the Latin *mandate*. "Mon-DAH-tay" is how he says it, like it's Spanish, but as soon as I write it out, I know what it means: mandate, law, command. He says the command this word *mandate* refers to is from Jesus' words to the disciples at the Last Supper:

> *I give you a new commandment, that you love one another. Just as I have loved you, you also should love one another.*

He says Jesus' love was wide and long and high and deep. His love took Him to the cross and the grave and the pit of hell. His love was costly.

I am tired of costly love. I ache with it. My eyes fill with it. My face is wet with it.

Jim says Jesus meets us in our tears, weeps with us, as he wept with Mary over the death of Lazarus. I suppose that should be comforting, and it is, but I'm tired of crying. I'm tired of aching. I'm tired of being met in brokenness and need. I'd like a little resurrection, thanks.

But it's not Easter yet.

And even if it were, we live our whole lives in the shadow of the Triduum, these three dark days before Easter, because the only way to resurrection is the way of death. I am fighting that hard. But even in my kicking against the goad, God meets me. That's what the pastors and theologians say anyway. That's what Jim says. He assures me that Jesus is with me, even in the midst of my frustration and lostness and pain. Jesus knows wilderness. He knows abandonment.

And he loves me that much, Jim says, that he's willing to come to the desert and the darkness when he could be enjoying eternal bliss at the right hand of the Father. And what else can we do, in the face of such love, Jim asks, but love one another as he has loved us? As he has commanded us?

I can fight it all I want—and I clearly do—but that's the Jesus way. That's the way I say I walk. Or at least say I want to walk. The way of costly love. That stuff I'm tired of. And I know the cost of love, for me, right now, is my fledgling writing career.

No! my heart cries. *I have an agent I was referred to! I was going to send her a query next week! I knew this is what would happen if we had a third baby. This is why I did not want a third baby!*

Yet here I sit, baby bump in my belly, and listen to the words of
Jesus. A new command. Love one another. As I have loved you. And I
know I must relinquish my dream of writing another book, of finding
an agent for my novel, of being a multi-published author. Those may
be works of love, but for a different time, another season. I have other
works of love right now: these two children I already have, this new
baby that is growing within me. My first work in this season is to love
my kids. And to love them well, I must let my dreams of publication
go.

Tears well in my eyes. This is my little cross to bear. I feel ridiculous
and melodramatic saying that. I feel even more ridiculous and melodramatic saying this: it doesn't seem so little.

But who am I kidding? I had negative book sales for the second half
of last year. No one is even reading the words I've already published; it's
not like I'm really giving anything up here.

So why does my heart hurt?

Jim invites us forward to receive the body and the blood. When
I stand, Jane lifts her arms to me. I pick her up and hold her on my
hip as I wait my turn in the silent line moving toward the front of the
sanctuary. Jim gives Jane a blessing, resting his hand on her hair. Then
he hands me a wafer. "Kimberlee," he says, "the body of Christ was
broken for you." I dip the wafer in the cup. "And the blood of Christ
was poured out for your sake."

I chew the juice-soaked wafer—the body and blood of Christ.

Jesus gave His very life—for spoiled, self-absorbed people like me, no
less. Surely I can give up my dreams of Authorhood for a few years. For
the sake of my children. For the sake of love.

I return to the third pew and sit down, Jane still in my arms. I kiss
her forehead. I blink back tears.

Good Friday
more mercy grace—squared

We had our 20-week ultrasound today. You know, the one where they take all the baby's measurements to find out if it has any chromosomal anomalies or health/medical issues. But really, it's the one when we get to find out if baby Olive is a boy or a girl. So there we all are in the ultrasound room—Doug, the kids, and me. The tech turns down the lights and starts moving his magic ultrasound wand over my bare belly.

Doug says, "All right, kids, last predictions: boy or girl?"

The tech says, "Looks like you can have a boy and a girl."

"What?" I say.

"You're having twins."

There's a moment of shocked silence. Then Doug laughs, his nervous oh-man-I'm-in-trouble-now laugh.

"You're kidding," I finally say.

Doug shakes his head. "He's not kidding. I can see both babies myself."

I stare at the screen, unable to process what I'm seeing.

"But—but that's impossible!" I feel like I'm dreaming, or underwater, or in a movie. This doesn't feel real. It can't be real.

But it is. Even I can tell that there are two babies floating around on that screen...which means there are two babies floating around inside of me.

"Oh my God," I say. "Are—are they Siamese?"

The tech laughs. "No. You can see the wall of the separate sacs here." He points to a thin white line that I can barely see.

To me, those two heads look conjoined. "Are you sure?"

He laughs again. "Very."

You'd think, being the worrywart I am, that I'd have considered this whole twin possibility a long time ago. And I did. But the in-office ultrasound at 11 weeks clearly showed just one baby.

Of course, lying here with wide eyes glued to the screen with those two babies clearly visible, I now remember that when the midwife did that initial ultrasound, she said, at the very end, "Wait a minute. That's odd," and started moving the ultrasound wand around my belly trying to see…something, I didn't know what. Anxiety flooded from my knees to the top of my head. She looked around a bit more as I lay there feeling like my world might be about to flip upside down, and then she said, "Okay, it's all fine. It must have just been a strange view across the placenta," and I expelled the breath I didn't know I'd been holding. She assured us that there was only one baby in there and sent us home with a very clear ultrasound picture of Baby Olive: and it's just Olive.

When I tell this to the tech, he grumbles, "They"—meaning the doctors and midwives—"shouldn't be allowed to have those"—meaning the Fisher Price ultrasound machines they use for office visits. Then he says, "Baby A's a boy."

I raise my eyebrows. We were pretty convinced Olive was a girl. "Are you sure?"

He points to the screen. "You can see his little penis for yourself."

And I can. I look at Jane. "Maybe the other one will be a girl."

She nods and holds my hand.

Back in January, when I told our home group I was pregnant, I jokingly added, "If it's a girl we're going to name her Mercy Grace, because that's what I'll need to parent three kids."

Elaine said, "What if it's a boy?"

Her husband, Tom, laughed. Every year on the church camp out, one of their two boys ends up in the emergency room. It's become a joke: it wouldn't be a church camping trip if one of the Helman boys didn't up in the hospital. Tom grinned at me and said, "Then you name him More Mercy Grace."

So here I lie with More Mercy Grace in my belly. I hold Jane's hand and hope hope hope the other twin is a girl.

It's not. I look at Doug with wide eyes. "What are we going to do?" I whisper. "It'll be like living with Jake and Charlie Helman."

"No," he says. "It won't be. It won't be."

I can only hope he's right. But he isn't even convinced he's right, which doesn't bode well for my future. "We have to move," I say. Our 800-square-foot house is not big enough for six people, especially not when half of them are growing boys. If these twins are anything like Jack, they'll be climbing the windows and doorframes before they're two.

Doug nods.

"Soon," I say, "before these boys get too big and rambunctious."

"Kimberlee," Doug says it soft, like he's about to break bad news to me, "before we can buy a new house, we need to buy a new car."

He's right of course. Three kids in car seats would be a squeeze in the back of our Accord. Four is impossible.

I look at the two little curled bodies floating around on the screen. I am going to be the mother of twins. I wasn't even sure I wanted three children, and here I'm going to have four? Ho. Lee. Crap. Four!

Lord have mercy. And grace. And more.

grace notes, april 2

The twins are healthy and developmentally normal.

They're not Siamese.

They're not triplets.

Or quads. (Thank you, dear Lord Jesus!)

I have good health insurance and excellent health care.

I found $1.05 in change in my purse and car yesterday—just enough to pay for parking!

Sunshine.

Charlotte's Web, which I'm reading to Jack and Jane. I haven't read it since third grade. E.B. White is a wonder.

A new bottle of ink for my fountain pen. I ran out last week and had to journal with a ball point (bleh).

My dishwasher. I'm so grateful to no longer be hand-washing dishes. And with twins on the way, I'm doubly grateful for this particular automation.

A trip to the library for new books to read.

The cup of tears Jesus drank for me, my children, everyone I love—because He loves them (and me) far more than I ever could.

And that the cup of tears did not have the last word. Jesus drank it to the dregs—and then He rose from the dead. I know it's still Lent, but: Hallelujah!

Holy Saturday
laid in the earth

I have this image of laying my writing career (career? is that what this is?)—and my beloved novel especially—in the earth with Jesus on this Holy Saturday. How long must it lie there?

When Laura and her kids come over this afternoon, I tell her about this, about how hard it is, about how much I wanted to send a query to this agent. "I have a referral," I explain. "The other agent I was referred to—she asked for a partial. I think this one will, too."

She shakes her head. "Don't do it. I know you want to, but don't." She places her hand gently on my arm. "You're going to have twins, Kimberlee. They're going to keep you so busy you won't have time to even think about your novel, let alone work on it."

I bristle. Her words feel dismissive, like some sort of final pronouncement handed down from the bench by a smooth-faced, chisel-jawed judge with long years of indifference etched into his demeanor. I know she doesn't mean it this way. I know she's being entirely rational. I even know she's right. But I was hoping for a little sympathy, a little oh-wow-this-not-writing-is-going-to-be-hard-on-you. But of course Laura doesn't understand. She's not a writer. She's a mother par excellence, the at-home kind who identifies herself as her kids' mom. She can't understand that I love my novel almost as much as I love my kids or that my not writing would be like her going blind and no longer being able to see Ryan play soccer or Ella's dance recitals. I need to stop talking about my writing with people who aren't writers. It just makes me feel bad about myself.

And it makes me mean. When Laura says I'm going to be too busy to even think about my writing, the eyes of my heart narrow and I think, *I'll show you. I'll revise my novel, write my magazine articles, blog every day, and have twins—and I'll do it all with one hand tied behind my back, you naysaying wet blanket.*

But my face smiles, and my mouth changes the subject, and when she leaves, I go to my room and cry.

Easter
a season of laughter
(april/may)

The sole way to put flight into the wing,
To preen its feathers, and to make them grow,
Is to heed humbly every smallest thing
With which the Christ in us has aught to do.

—George MacDonald, *Diary of an Old Soul*

april fool

When I called my mom on Friday afternoon and told her that we were having twins, she said, "You're kidding!"

Come to think of it, that's what pretty much everyone has said. Well, except for my friend Carrie, who asked Doug, "Has Kimberlee stopped crying yet?" And Susan, who texted back, "OMG!!!" (This from Susan; in 13 years of friendship, I have never, ever heard her take the Lord's name in vain—until now.) And Tiffany, who said, "You can do this, Kimberlee. You can." I have to believe her. She's living through the hell of having a month-old baby and a five-year-old with leukemia. If she can do that, I can do twins. Not that either of us has much choice.

Actually, my mom didn't just say, "You're kidding!"

First, she screeched, "Whaaat?" I held the phone away from my ear. Then she screeched, "Twins?! You're kidding!"

"Oh, I only wish I were."

Then, suspiciously, "Is this some kind of April Fool's joke?"

"April Fool's was yesterday," I said.

When I finally convinced her, she said, "Well, sweetie, twins do run in the family."

"Please, Mama," I said, "Grandpa's sisters hardly count. These babies are fraternal anyway. That sort of thing passes down from mother to daughter. You couldn't have gotten that trait from Grandpa."

She didn't understand. And once she did, we spent several minutes arguing over whether it was *fraternal* or *paternal*. I think we're both going deaf because it turns out we were both saying "fraternal."

"What does that mean anyway?" she asked.

"It means I dropped two eggs, and Doug's nasty little sperm fertilized both of them."

She laughed so hard I thought she would fall over. But she was probably sitting down already.

"When do you need me?" she said when she could breathe again. "And for how long?"

"When can you come?" I said. "How long can you stay?"

She agreed to come in early August, since twins almost always come early and it was unlikely I'd make it to my actual due date on the 24th—unless I needed her sooner. And she'd stay through mid-September. Now we just need to find her a place to stay, since she doesn't want to sleep in our basement with the mice. Though she would, if that were her only option. She's generous to a fault, my mama.

the name game

We thought Baby Olive would be a girl. Doug and I have a raft of girl names. We have just one boy name. It took a long time for us to agree on that one. And now we have to come up with another. So we've been asking around for boy names that people really like.

My sister has been the most helpful in this regard. "I came up with names for the boys," she tells me. I have the phone on speaker while I chop onions for the pasta sauce. "I am officially submitting my request for Linus and Archibald."

"Over my dead body," Doug hollers from the living room.

Jen hollers back, "Will you go for Luke and Han?"

"No!" Doug says.

I say, "I was thinking Bo and Luke. Or Hans and Franz."

"Nah," Jen says, "but how about Edward and Jacob?" Jen belongs to the Edward-Cullen-has-ruined-me-for-mortal-men Facebook group.

"I've never even read *Twilight*," I say. "Besides, I'd take Colin Firth in a wet shirt over pretty boy Edward any day. How about we call them Darcy and Bingley?"

From the living room, Doug calls out, "Over my dead body."

I lean through the doorway to look at him. "You keep saying that. I do not think it means what you think it means."

Jen pretends not to hear this conversation. "Oooh," she says, "go with Charles and Fitzwilliam. No, wait. Doug will see through that. How about Charles and William? They're both family names, so that's a plus. You could totally play that angle. And at least Will wouldn't have my last name: Will Barrow. That's just cruel."

I snort and get a nose full of onion fumes. "Now look what you've done," I say through my coughing and tears. "You've gone and made the pregnant lady cry."

We laugh together, so hard that I have to lean on the counter for support, and it feels like a huge gift, this laughter—because Carrie was right when she asked if I'd stopped crying yet. I did cry on Good Friday. And Holy Saturday, too. My world has flipped upside-down, and the future I'd planned for myself has evaporated as surely as my hope for book royalties. And it sucks. Hard. And yet—I laugh with my sister over the boys' names. I don't yet realize that laughing in the face of fear or adversity or the upending of life as you know it is a form of triumph. For now, I just know that regardless of whether I laugh or cry, my life is going to be a whole different beast than I thought—and that laughing feels whole lot better than crying.

Later, after I get off the phone with Jen, I ask Doug, "How about Charles and William?"

"Over my dead body," he says.

***

A week later, we take the Question of the Boys' Names to our home group. Seven of us sit in the living room of Carrie and Rick's house, and I tell them, "Doug's mother thinks since we already have two kids named John we should just go with it."

"Two kids named John?" says Carrie.

"Jack's given name," I say, "is really John. And Jane is the feminine form of John. Doug's mom suggested Juan and Ian."

Our friend John, who is Jane's godfather, says, "Juan? I don't think so. Your white baby will look more like a Johann."

Carrie says, "Or if he has Doug's coloring, maybe a Gianni?"

I pretend to be oblivious to the fact that others are speaking and continue my monologue. "I actually like the name Ian, but Ian Ireton sounds like a super hero's day name."

Sprague, who loves comic books, says, "You should name them Clark and Kent!"

Rick chimes in. "Peter and Parker!"
John says, "Bruce and Wayne!"
And it continues to devolve:
Sprague: "Starsky and Hutch!"
Rick: "Simon and Simon!"
Doug: "Darrell and Darrell!"
Me: "Over my dead body."

another bad day

Today is a bad day. Another one. To add to the slough of grumpy days I've had lately. Only today is worse.

I wake up at 3 a.m. with a raging head cold and can't get back to sleep, and when the kids wake up, they're both a little under the weather and cranky, too. Jack fusses all through his morning chores. I yell at him. Jane throws a fit when I ask her to get ready to go to the gym. I yell at her. When I get to the gym for my prenatal yoga class, I realize I've mixed up the times and shown up just as it ended. I yell at myself —inside my head, of course; I'm not so far gone as to start talking to myself out loud. Yet.

But make lemonade, right? (And I'm soooo good at that.) Since it's sunny, I take the kids to the park. Jack lies on the bench the entire time we're there, says his tummy hurts. So we come home, and suddenly he feels fine—fine enough to run around the house with his Lego starship and scream the Darth Vader theme at the top of his lungs, while his sister runs away from him, shrieking. I yell that I have a headache and go to your room and be quiet! NOW!

My babysitter calls and says she's sick, and won't be able to come in the afternoon, which means I'm not going to be able to meet with my spiritual director, and on this day of all days, I could really use some spiritual direction.

At 4:30, Laura, who's supposed to come over for dinner with her kids, calls to say they won't be coming after all—Ella and Ryan are sick, too.

At 5, Doug calls and says he won't be home at 7 like he thought but closer to 8:30. I hang up on him.

At 7:45, instead of staying in their beds, Jack and Jane start chasing each other around the house screaming like banshees. I completely lose my head and yell at them—again—and then I start weeping, terrified by the prospect of adding two more children to my life. I can't handle two kids. What am I going to do with four?

Jack and Jane creep back to bed and stay there, quiet. I feel like a jerk.

The pity party I've been having all day gives way to self-loathing, and the nasty voices in my head get really loud: "Oh, the poor privileged princess didn't have her nanny today. Wah. She has two healthy young children and is pregnant with two more. We should play our tiny violin for her, poor thing. To have so much abundance when some people who want children can't have them, and some people who have them don't have the means to care for them—it must be rough, this life she lives." And on and on until I feel about as big as a mung bean and want to crawl into bed and never get out.

And then, by the grace of God, I remember something that Emily Barrett wrote in one of her books: the only way to get out of this nasty spiral of self-loathing and self-pity is to get the focus off myself and to look outward, look upward. I stare out the kitchen window as I rinse the dinner dishes, and I pray.

"Thank you, God, for warm water. For my dishwasher. For my children. For my husband who will be home any moment. Thank you that you don't see me the way the voices in my head see me, that you love me even on days like today, when I feel utterly unlovable…"

The list of things to be grateful for goes on and on, until by the time I go to bed, I feel okay, like maybe the day hasn't been a complete loss, like maybe there is hope for me, for my kids, for our family, our future.

Maybe. But oh God, two more kids? Really?

surrender to the dark side

We bought a car. Not just any car. A minivan. Yes, it's true. I am now a mom with a minivan. Next thing you know I'll be signing my kids up for soccer.

I did not want to buy a new car, least of all a minivan. For one thing, I am not a fan of minivans. For another, I love my Accord. But there's no way four children will fit into our Accord. Not unless we strap Jack to the roof with bungee cords. He'd probably enjoy that, but I have a feeling it's illegal.

I had hoped we could get a Pilot—anything is better than a minivan, even an SUV wannabe—but once I actually looked at it, I realized four car seats would be a squeeze, and grocery shopping would be a nightmare with that tiny trunk. And where would I put the stupid double stroller I'm going to have to have?

The minivan has become inevitable. But I'm not happy about it.

Who could be? I have to give up my sexy silver Accord (hey, it has a stick shift, okay?) for a big clunky car that doesn't even have the *option* of a manual transmission. Loser vehicle. Not to mention, it's about as fun to drive as a sofa. A nice sofa. But still.

And the crowning insult is that I will be paying hundreds of dollars a month for the next five years for the dubious privilege of driving a couch-car and being a cliché: Kimberlee, the minivan-driving soccer mom. Oh God, have I really sunk this far?

fleeing ahead

After church on Sunday, I'm chatting with Carrie and Rick when Rick notices a rash on my arm and neck. Being an oncologist and all, he says, "You know, sometimes people get a rash like that when they have a low platelet count."

I brush it off, saying I had a rash much like it when I was pregnant with Jane.

That afternoon, I work for a bit in the yard, pruning our out-of-control mock orange tree. When I stop after 40 minutes (okay, it might have been 50, *maybe* an hour), I notice that the veins in my hands and arms are swollen to twice their normal size, bulging grotesquely through my skin—and the rash stands out in stark and scary red relief against the blue of my veins.

As I stare at my hands and forearms, all bulging blue veins and tiny red spots against pale, pale skin, I remember Rick's comment about the platelet count and I just know I have leukemia or multiple myeloma and that we won't be able to treat it till after the babies are born and by then it will be too late because I'll die mere days after the twins' birth, like some sort of real life Elizabeth Penderwick, and Jack and Jane will be devastated and their little hearts will break and poor Doug will be left alone with four children, two of them just babies, and I won't get to see my children grow up and my twins won't even remember me, and I am embarrassed to admit this, but hypochondriac freak that I am, I actually believe myself. I actually *cry*.

Sometimes, having a vivid imagination is a curse.

When I wake this morning, it's once more grabbing me by the heart, this fear that I'm dying. I know it's irrational. But you can't reason with irrational fear. It just is. And boy, this morning, it *really* is.

I'm certain that rash means I have cancer. When I mention this to Doug over breakfast and tell him what Rick said, my way-too-rational husband kindly points out that I have no other symptoms.

"I'm tired, fatigued," I say.

He raises his eyebrows. "You're pregnant with twins. And you're assuming that low platelet count can only be caused by cancer."

I have to admit he's right about that one.

So clearly, I'm irrational and a hypochondriac. But we already knew that. And knowing that doesn't really help me stop being irrational and a hypochondriac. It just makes me feel stupid as well as afraid.

I wash the breakfast dishes. I review addition facts with Jack. I cuddle on the sofa with both kids and read them a couple chapters from *Little House in the Big Woods*. And I feel anxious and idiotic the whole time.

Then, while the kids are off playing with their Legos and Polly Pockets in their bedroom, I plop myself onto the sofa and pick up the Emily Barrett book I'm reading. It takes me awhile to get over my anxiety enough to focus on her words, but when I do, five of them leap off the page at me: "Fear is the fleeing ahead." My eyes widen, and I read those words again. "Fear is the fleeing ahead." And I realize that's exactly what I'm doing: feeling afraid not because the present is scary but because the future is or, rather, might be; because I'm trying to guess and prepare for The Next Bad Thing.

But in truth, my life at this particular moment is good, and I'm missing out on its goodness, on God's presence in the present because I am fleeing ahead.

I stop running. I sit in the moment and stare at the book, at those words, and say thank you God for this moment and these words that I needed to hear.

Then, of course, I email my OB to ask about low platelet count.

She emails back and says it sometimes occurs in late pregnancy and has nothing to do with cancer. She says she'll order a blood test at my visit next week if I want it, not because she thinks it's necessary but just to ease my mind. I like that about her.

And each time the fear comes today, I try to remember Emily's words. I try to return to the moment at hand and notice the blessings of that moment:

Tulips blooming everywhere, and Jane's exuberant cry of "Tulip!" every time she sees one on our walk.

The delicious scent of lilac blossoms.

Listening to Jack and Jane play: the Little Mermaid is fighting Darth Vader.

Rhubarb-apple crisp.

God-blesses and blessings, hugs and snuggles at bedtime.

It's not a perfect day, but it ends up being a whole lot better than I thought possible this morning. Three cheers for gratitude and grace and God.

the weigh they grow

I've been reading about nutrition and weight gain for a twin pregnancy. Apparently, you don't need to gain an extra 8 or 10 pounds for that extra baby; you need to gain an extra 25 or 30. It's like being two pregnant women instead of just one.

Luckily, I'm well on my way to packing on the requisite 60 pounds during this pregnancy. When I weighed myself at the gym after yoga today, I discovered I've gained 28 pounds in 22 weeks! No wonder my body creaks and groans like a haunted house.

The other woman in my yoga class? She's 20 weeks pregnant—and you can't even tell. But me? At 22 weeks I look like a frigging freighter. I no longer have a waist; I have an anti-waist—my belly has expanded into two small bulges where my waist used to be. With Jack and Jane, all my pregnancy momentum was forward. Apparently twins also grow out your sides, like tumors.

To get to this oh-so-desirable state, I'm on this high-protein, high-calorie diet that most people can only dream about. Here's what I'm supposed to eat every day:

- 8 cups of milk or yogurt (or 8 hefty slices of cheese)
- 4 cups of vegetables
- 4 cups of fruit
- 10 cups of cooked grains or cereal (or 10 slices of bread)
- 2 eggs
- 9 ounces of meat, fish, or poultry, at least 6 of which should be beef or pork

And 16 cups of water, which, if you do the math, turns out to be a whole gallon, which is a lot for anyone, let alone someone who has two babies sitting on her bladder.

In order to get all this food crammed down my throat, I eat all the time—every two hours, whether I'm hungry or not.

Can I whine for just a moment and say I am *so sick* of eating?

And I'm not one of those chicks who doesn't actually like food, either. I love food. There are few things in life that I like more than good food. A good book, maybe, and a good conversation with a good friend—both of which are made even better when paired with good food.

But too much of a good thing is still too much.

Tonight, while I sit at the dining room table and digest my quarter-pound burger with all the fixings, Doug pulls out the blender and makes me my after-dinner milkshake—16 ounces of milk and ice cream and cocoa powder. He sets it down on the table beside me. "Drink up."

I put my head on my arms and moan. "I don't want it." I'm still full from the seven meals I've already eaten today. But I'm a good girl. It takes me half an hour, but I drink the whole thing.

I sure hope these babies appreciate the sacrifices I'm making for them.

grace notes, may 7

As we leave the library after story time this morning, Jane says, "Mama, I want to hold your hand." And she slips her soft little hand into mine. Then I glance across the street and see the reader board outside St. Luke's. It reads "God is good."

My OB calls this afternoon: my platelet count is fine. (But I'm anemic. Apparently the six ounces of beef I'm eating every day isn't enough to keep me in iron. Time to go gnaw on a skillet.)

Doug and Jack make delicious oatmeal raisin cookies for me after dinner, simply because I want them. While they bake, Jane draws a picture of Doug that makes me laugh: he looks like a paramecium.

After cookies and milk, I lie in bed obsessing over every ominous ache and pain in my body. Jack comes in and asks me to check his pajamas because something is poking him under his arm. I tell you what: there's nothing like a prosaic moment of armpit searching to make you forget your fear.

A gossamer thin crescent moon hangs in the western sky, Venus just above it, shining pure and bright.

St. Luke's is right: God is very, very good.

the watermelon

Sometime between my going to bed last night and waking up this morning, my belly grew. Again. Exponentially.

It is now roughly the size of a watermelon. And not just any watermelon. A Biggest-Size-Prize-winning watermelon at the county fair.

When I go to the gym for my prenatal yoga class, I decide that, since I have a watermelon sitting on my bladder, I had best go to the ladies' room before I go to class. The old-people's swim class must have just gotten out because I am the only woman under 70 in the room. Most of the old ladies are happily changing in the locker room, but two more modest souls decide to use the two bathroom stalls.

I wait for them to be done.

And wait.

And wait.

After about five minutes of standing there with my legs crossed, I seriously consider yelling, "Hey! Get a move on! There's a pregnant lady here who needs to pee!" But my mama raised me to respect my elders, so I keep my trap shut, glower at the stall doors, and leave.

The other women's bathroom at the gym is on the third floor, so I huff up two flights of stairs, the watermelon bouncing gracelessly against my bladder. Thank God for panty liners.

As I round the second floor landing, a guy passes me. "Hoo, girl. You look like you're about to pop!" he says. "What are you? Nine months?"

I smile weakly. "Six and a half."

His eyebrows shoot up.

"I'm having twins."

His eyebrows shoot up more. "I got five kids. Ain't none of 'em twins. I don't envy you. You're gonna have your hands full."

"Yes," I say and continue wheezing up the last few steps to the locker room. It disturbs me to realize that the watermelon I'm carrying around really is as big as I think it is. I tend to magnify problems, and knowing this about myself allows me to dismiss them, to say things like, "Oh, it's really not as bad as I think." But apparently, at least this time, it is as bad as I think.

After using the ladies' facilities, I look at the watermelon in the mirror. It's hard to imagine that it's going to get even bigger. But I've still got 11 weeks to go, so it will get bigger. Only God knows how much.

After yoga, I call my sister to tell her about my watermelon. I say, "Just to be on the safe side, maybe I should invest in a walker with a sling between the handles. The sling can hold up my belly. And the walker can hold up the rest of me."

"Good idea," she says. "Better get a motorized one."

crusader

Most Monday nights, our friend Sprague comes over for dinner. Uncle Sprague, the kids call him, and after dinner they always beg him to play Giant Octopus. Tonight is no exception. Sprague looks at me. "Is that okay?"

"Sure," I say, "as soon as they're ready for bed." Jack and Jane run to their room, already stripping off their shirts as they scoot through the doorway. "Teeth brushed, too!" I call after them.

Three minutes later, they present themselves in pajamas with their teeth brushed. Sprague raises his arms—only now they're tentacles—and says, "I'm going to eat you!" They squeal and dash to their room.

Doug and I start washing the dinner dishes and listen to the mayhem.

Jack growls and Jane roars as Sprague attacks them with his giant tentacles.

"Take that!" Jack shouts with another roar.

Sprague fake screams. "Ack! You cut off one of my tentacles. Aaaack!" I hear him stumbling around the room. Then his tone changes. "Bwahaha! But you forget! I'm the Giant Octopus, and my tentacles regenerate!"

Then there's lots of inarticulate squealing and shrieking as Jack and Jane scramble to get away from Sprague, who's roaring loudly.

Suddenly, in the midst of this cacophony, Jane screams, "Save us, O God! Kill him!"

In the kitchen Doug and I both laugh out loud. He says drily, "Thus began the Crusades."

***

A week later, I sit in the comfier of the two chairs in the little room off of Margie's back porch, the room I've been coming to for spiritual direction once a month for seven years. After she prays, Margie asks her standard opening salvo. "So, where has God been meeting you?"

I shake my head. "I don't know, Margie. All this is so overwhelming. The twins. The changes they'll bring. I'm grateful they're healthy, grateful I'm healthy, grateful Doug and Jack and Jane are all healthy."

She waits quietly.

Thinking of Jane, I smile as I remember her screaming "Save us, O God! Kill him!"

"I'm grateful for laughter." I tell Margie about Jane's comment, and she laughs, which makes me laugh. Then I tell her about the stupid baby hugger lift I'm going to be getting. "It's a kind of girdle," I say, "for shoring up my watermelon." I describe this get-up to her, and pretty soon we're both laughing so hard the tears are streaming and I nearly pee. Luckily I'm sitting down, so I just cross my legs a little tighter.

"Oh man," I say, "I have to stop laughing. I'm going to pee my pants." Then I start laughing harder, remembering a week or so ago after I came home from the grocery store, and I actually did. "I was standing on the porch, with a grocery bag in one hand and my keys in the other, and I sneezed twice, right in a row, really fast. There was nowhere to sit down, no time to cross my legs, and pee just dribbled right down the inside of my thigh!"

Margie's laughing through the whole story.

"I'm just grateful I was at home, you know? So I could change right away. I just hope this isn't permanent, that it goes away after the babies are born. I don't want to be wearing diapers as well as changing them."

She laughs harder still. "Oh, Kimberlee," she says. "Don't you see?"

"See what?" I say. "That I'm destined for incontinence?"

She laughs. "No, don't you see God?"

"God?"

"Yes, God! I see God in all of this laughter. So clearly. I see his delight in your laughter. I see you growing: you got handed one heck of a lemon, and look at you laughing in the face of it!"

"Well," I say, "I cry, too. Just for the record."

She nods. "I know. But you're laughing right now. And you laughed over all these stories you told me. Don't you see how wonderful that is?" She smiles and then adds, "It's still Easter. I think it's just perfect that this season of laughter in your life is happening during Easter."

I hadn't thought of that. Though I'm not exactly rejoicing in the fact that I'll soon be the mother of four children, I am laughing—a lot—about the absurdity of it all. I'm laughing about the crazy changes to my body, laughing with Jack and Jane over Pa's encounter with the stump he thought was a bear in *Little House in the Big Woods*, laughing with Doug over the unbelievable things the kids say. Margie is right: all this laughter seems very appropriate in this season. I cried the first few days—Good Friday and Holy Saturday—as my expectations for my life were once more re-ordered or, rather, overturned, but then, miracle of miracles, I began to laugh.

I tell Margie, "Anne Lamott says that laughter is carbonated holiness."

"I like that," she says, and smiles. "Carbonated holiness. Yes."

Ordinary Time
girth
(june/july)

…being great with child.

—*The Gospel of Luke*

accord

Doug lists our car on Craigslist on Wednesday, and I pray with uncharacteristic boldness, "God, please let it sell by Monday. Preferably by Saturday." And, lo and behold, it does.

Of course, on Saturday afternoon, when the new owner drives my beloved Accord away, I cry. Be careful what you pray for, eh?

My tears surprise everyone, especially me. I know we need to sell the car. I had been bugging Doug for over a week to get it listed. I had prayed it would sell. And then I go and get all weepy about it.

I try to laugh as I wipe my eyes and nose on my sleeve. After all, it's just a car.

But it was a good car. My first car. And it represents my life as it has been, and I really love my life, so watching it pull away from the curb and drive off never to return is sort of symbolic: my life is about to change, and it will never be the same, and I'm grieving the loss of this life I love.

Oh, I know my life with four children will still be good. I know it will be rich and full and all that. But it will be different, and I've never adapted to change easily, even good change.

I probably should have had some sort of good-bye ceremony for the Accord. Not that the car would have cared, but it might have helped me.

As I sit here on the front porch, weeping and laughing at myself for weeping, Doug holds up the stack of hundred dollar bills that the buyer brought and waves them in front of me. I've never seen so much cash at one time in my life. It feels like drug money. Or blood money. I cry harder, even as I laugh at myself for being such a dork.

But within the hour I pull myself together and drive the sofa-mobile to the credit union and deposit the stack o' cash into our account. Then I go home and do something really sexy with it: I pad our emergency fund and throw the rest at our loan on the stupid minivan.

Maybe I should have kept a hundred bucks and bought a commemorative plaque for the Accord, to hang in the driveway—a small reminder of a life I no longer have.

girdle

Because of the watermelon I'm carrying in place of what used to be my waist, I've been feeling a lot of pressure on my bladder and my pelvic floor. This is a pain, almost literally, in the patookiss. Also, what with the gallon of water I'm drinking every day, it means I have to pee, like, every 24 minutes.

So a few weeks ago my OB ordered me a little thingamajig called a Baby Hugger Lift. It arrives in the mail today, and I immediately strip off my prego jeans and t-shirt to put it on. This—uh, *contraption* is really the only word for it—is an elasticized girdle, like something your great-grandma Gertrude would have worn, to which you attach suspenders, like your great-grandpa Fred's, to which you attach an elastic band that runs under your belly thereby transferring the weight of the watermelon off your pelvic floor and onto your shoulders so that walking is slightly more comfortable.

Yeah, just try taking that get-up off every 24 minutes when you have to use the ladies' room.

Luckily, the designers thought of everything: there's a little piece of Velcro attached to the crotch of this thing, so I don't have to remove the whole kit-and-caboodle every time I have to pee; I just have to unvelcro the crotch. The first time I use it, the Velcro falls into the toilet.

I guess the designers didn't quite think of *every*thing.

I already felt like a pinheaded beached whale. Now I feel like a pinheaded beached whale wearing her grandmother's girdle.

To add injury to insult, while the Baby Hugger Lift does actually lift my belly off my cervix and make it marginally more comfortable to walk, it also lifts my belly into my lungs, making it more difficult to breathe. And it's June, so in about three weeks when the weather turns warm, wearing this thick, elasticized get-up is going to roast me alive.

But at least no one is going to see me in it. Well, except Doug. When I undress for bed tonight, he takes one look at my new girdle and says, "Wow. Uh, wow. I'm—I have nothing to say."

Thank you. I'm going to go crawl in a hole now. I just have to find one big enough to hold my watermelon.

green

I read a blog post this morning by a woman who is a senior partner in a law firm, the mother of three young children, a Sunday school teacher, an avid cook and hostess of gourmet dinner parties, a voracious reader, and the author of a newly published novel.

I hate her the moment I read her post.

And I hereby vow never to read her book, let alone buy it. I mean, jeez, it's not like I need to feel more crappy about myself. I spend so much time and energy giving myself pep talks to try to convince me that I'm okay even though I stay home with our kids, even though my book is a flop, even though 20 agents have passed on my novel, even though a mere handful of people read my blog, even though I feel like a beached whale most of the time these days—scarcely able to breathe, let alone change position, get back in the water, and swim. So. I do not appreciate this woman. I do not admire her. And I do not care to read her book which, if it's anything like her blog post, will only make me feel like a crap-covered beached whale.

Or a crap-filled one. I feel very small and petty and jealous right now. I try to comfort myself with the knowledge that this superwoman can't possibly spend much time with her kids, who will probably grow up to be serial killers, whereas my children with whom I spend nearly every waking moment will, I tell Doug, be doctors, pastors, teachers, and CEO's of Fortune 500 companies devoted to serving the world's poor.

Doug says, "There is no such thing as a Fortune 500 company that makes money serving the poor."

I say, "It's my fantasy. I can make up whatever I want."

He laughs and says, "I love you, you know that?"

I do. And I'm so grateful, because right now, I feel pretty ugly and unlovable, in so many ways.

Later, in bed, I realize this woman probably has a nanny—a full-time one—and a housekeeper, too. It's not likely she's doing everything I'm doing plus being a lawyer plus writing a book. Right?

I also wonder why I care, why this post has tweaked me so much that I've gone all green-eyed and catty. I am trying to justify myself to this woman with her Type A go-get-'em, take-no-prisoners personality, trying to get someone like her to approve of—or at least sympathize with—someone like me. But why? Superwoman has critical eyes. Or oblivious ones. If she saw me at all, she'd brush me aside. I'm not important enough to waste more than a single critical glance on before she passes me by on her way to God-knows-where. Purgatory, I hope.

I remember Anne Lamott's words about seeing herself through the tender eyes of Jesus and Mary instead of through the critical eyes of the men at the Belvedere Tennis Club. And that's what I need: to get to a place where Jesus stands between me and the critical eyes of the superwomen of this world, between me and my own critical eyes, because let's face it, Superwoman doesn't know I exist, and all my ideas about her are projections. I need Jesus to stand in the gap between who I am and how I see myself, so I can see His eyes instead of my own, and see that they are full of love and delight, that He looks at me the way Doug looks at me, the way Susan and Tiffany and Margie look at me, the way I look at my children. I need to see myself reflected in Jesus' eyes as someone who is deeply loved, liked, even admired, despite my foibles, failures, and flaws, despite my small-minded jealousy and self-doubt and all the rest of it.

Jesus loves me; I believe this. Now, I simply need to get out of my own way, quit looking at myself, and focus on Him, so I can see His love and delight in me and let it sink in, soak in, fill me. Then the superwomen of the world can rush on their hurried way, and I can dawdle on mine, and it won't matter.

I feel so much better after thinking all this that I actually pray for Superwoman, for the success of her book, and that God would help her to slow down so she doesn't miss quite so much on this road of writing and motherhood.

It's a very smug, self-satisfied sort of prayer.

grace notes, june 4

I get to pick up Susan at the airport today. After five years, she's home to stay. Yay and hallelujah!

A playdate with Madeline, Michaela, and baby Emily this morning. Tiffany and I get to catch up, and Michaela is well enough to play with Jane.

Before nap time, the kids and I finish reading *Rapunzel's Revenge*— again. I love how much they love it.

While Jane and I nap, Jack begins writing a book about a boy named George who is seeking a treasure so he can afford to buy a bigger house. The picture of the bigger house shows rooms with bookcases filled with books. My lit-lover's soul is content as with marrow and fatness.

When I'm tucking Jane in tonight, after we've said God-blesses and her blessing, she informs me, "The Holy Spirit is Jesus with us in our hearts, so even though Jesus is far away in Heaven, He's still with us." Amen. Amen.

For a whole 24 hours, I have not been dreaming up nasty, vengeful fates for Superwoman. In fact, I've hardly thought of her. Thank you, Jesus.

the cankle

I thought the Baby Hugger get-up was bad, but this? This is much worse: on Thursday evening, my ankles swell to the size of footballs. I look like my grandma. If it weren't so insanely ludicrous, I'd cry. Instead, I write a blog post:

> *Are you pregnant? Are you walking around on skinny, bony ankles that are no longer big enough to support your growing frame?*
>
> *Well, have no fear. The solution is at hand. It's called... The Cankle!*
>
> *Straight from the pages of* Fat Pregnancy, *this brand spanking new invention is half-calf, half-ankle: it extends your calf straight down to the bottom of your foot and is therefore far stronger and sturdier than those flimsy ankle bones you've been sporting for years.*
>
> *How, you ask, can you get one? Well, I happen to have a brand new pair—just got them this week!—and out of the goodness of my heart, I will lend them to the first person to respond to this post.*
>
> *In fact, I am so impressed with this new development in my pregnancy that I will happily* give *my cankles away. And you can keep them. Forever. Really. I don't want them back.*

So far, only one person has commented on this post—my sister, who says: "So, I am the first to comment... but joke's on you, missy! Can't send those things my way. I already have a pair." Drat. Looks like I'm stuck with these things.

the holy ordinary

Doug has taken Jack for a bike ride, and Jane is napping. It's a perfect Sunday afternoon: quiet, and I'm alone. Only I'm not alone—there are two babies doing the rumba on my bladder. I sit on the sofa, my journal open on my lap, and stare out the window. I feel restless, like I ought to be doing something, but my body won't let me. I just got winded climbing the stairs from the basement—and that was *after* I'd napped for an hour.

So I got out my journal, thinking that I would write, but I'm so tired I can't even think what to say to the page. My life feels bereft of things to write about, other than the babies and how tired they're making me and how sad I feel that my novel is lying in the basement collecting dust. And honestly? I'm tired of writing about that day after day after day.

Last week, when I met with Margie, she asked me (of course) where God's been meeting me lately.

I told her, "I feel like jotting down the grace notes is helpful, like it's a good, important discipline for me. It helps me to not be so anxious, which is huge, but—" I shrugged "—I wonder if it's really enough? I mean, a lot of the time, these things I'm writing down don't *feel* like grace. They feel like they could happen to anyone, you know? Which doesn't mean it's not grace. I know it is. But—" I shrugged again "—it just doesn't feel like it, so I don't feel particularly grateful for them. And I certainly don't feel joyful, the way all those verses say you should: rejoice in the Lord always and all that. I mostly just feel tired."

I paused for a moment. I wanted to say, "And I feel angry that because of these babies, I'm not able to write as much as I'd like."

I wanted to say, "I feel like this whole year of trying to find an agent for my novel was wasted."

But after my conversation with Laura on Holy Saturday, when she so flippantly dismissed my need to write, I hadn't wanted to talk about that with anyone. I didn't feel able to hear any more words that dismissed this ache I felt, and still feel, that minimized how much I'm going to miss writing, that implied I'm silly or lacking perspective because I mourn this laying down of my novel and my dreams for only God knows how long.

So I didn't say that. I said, "I feel—" I searched for a safer word than *angry* "—disappointed. And discouraged. I'm having a hard time letting go of my writing dreams, you know? And I feel like it shouldn't be this hard, like I should just buck up and deal."

Margie's voice was gentle when she spoke. "Kimberlee," she said, "you're pregnant. With twins. Of course you're tired. And it's always hard to give up a dream. Don't be too hard on yourself." She looked out the window a second. "And you know, N.T. Wright often translates the word *rejoice* as *celebrate*. Celebrate in the Lord always. Maybe that distinction will help you."

I gave her my best I'm-tracking-with-you look, but really, I wasn't tracking. She waited for me to say something, so I had to say, "I'm sorry. I don't understand what the difference is."

"Oh, I don't know that there's much of a difference in what the words mean. I just think that joy sounds to our postmodern ears like an emotion, something you *feel*, whereas celebration is something you *do*. And since you can't change how or what you feel—it's not like you can force yourself to feel joy—it might be better to focus on what you do, on how you're actually living, rather than what you're feeling or not feeling."

She is so wise.

"So," she continued, "how do you celebrate? How do you recognize the holiness in the ordinary?" She smiled. "Or maybe just how do you see God in the midst of your tiredness and disappointment?"

As I sit here on the sofa and stare out the window at the spirea, I ponder Margie's questions. A bee buzzes around the tip of a spirea branch and lights on the top leaf.

I know this is just a season, and a relatively short one—but I'm still frustrated by my lack of energy. I'm still frustrated that my brain feels like a sieve and that after about noon I can barely string six words together to form a coherent sentence. I'm frustrated that given this blessed hour of silence and aloneness, all I can do is sit on the sofa and stare at a bee on a leaf.

I want to cry. It's so frustrating to feel so stuck, so exhausted, so mentally enervated. But really, crying is too much effort. So I watch the bee. It buzzes down to a lower leaf. At least, I assume it's buzzing. I can't actually hear it.

What I do hear are Julianne's words to me this morning. She's our children's minister, and she cornered me on the stair landing after church as I was heaving my way up to Jane's Sunday School classroom. "Oh, Kimberlee," she said, "I read something this week that made me think of you. The author was talking about how sometimes people have two vocations that seem to conflict with each other, like they're working at cross-purposes. And I thought of you, because I know it's hard that you're not writing much right now." She put her arm around my shoulders. "This author said that eventually those two conflicting vocations would flow together, and both vocations would be stronger because of the other one." She smiled. Beamed, really. "And I just knew that passage was meant for you. I just knew—I know—that your mothering will make you a better writer, and your writing will make you a better mom." She gave me a hug. "So hang in there. They're going to come together."

The bee flies away, disappearing among the fig leaves, and I sit with Julianne's words.

Come tomorrow, I'll have eleven weeks till I'm full-term. And eleven weeks after that to get my sea legs on this crazy voyage of parenting twins. And eleven more weeks after that before I'm able to get enough sleep to think clearly and have energy for anything other than feeding and changing these babies and loving on Jack and Jane. That's 33 weeks—the better part of a year. It feels like an eternity from this side, but it's not. It's not.

I remember Lynne's email shortly after I'd told her about the twins. She commiserated, "I know that having two more babies will be hard for you, if only because it means you cannot write as much as you'd like to."

I emailed back: "This not-writing is my little cross to bear, my act of self-sacrificing love. I know you'll understand and not think me melodramatic for saying that. It's a small cross, I know, but it's hard for me."

She responded, "Writing is who you are, Kimberlee. I think not writing very much will be more than a little cross to bear. I think it will be a pretty big cross." And then she wrote, "But I know that you will write many, many things in your life, even books someday, and that God will use these babies to make you a better person—and a better writer."

I think God might be trying to tell me something through these women in my life.

Still, it's hard to be patient, to look ahead and see that it'll be many months before I have energy and brain cells to write the way I'm used to writing. But I can keep railing against it, or I can practice patience and take good notes and pay attention and not be in a hurry. I can learn to trust that in time God will provide an audience for my books—whatever they may be—and provide the time and energy and clarity of thought to write those books. I can learn to look to the future with hope rather than fear. And even in this agony of waiting, I can attend to the present moment and live in it, grateful for its gifts of bees and spirea branches.

If God can teach me patience through this, or teach me to wait on divine timing, or teach me to trust…well, much as I hate being a blob, at least I'll be a growing blob—and not just physically. While my body turns into a ponderous house, my soul could turn into something like a garden. Or a tree, with abundant fruit—the fruit of the Spirit, especially patience and possibly peace. Eventually.

And if that happens, Julianne and Lynne are right: mothering will make me a better writer. Or at the very least it will make me a better person. Which is probably more important.

From somewhere in the fig tree, I hear a bird. I pick up my jounal and write down the bee and the birdsong. I don't know what they mean, but they're graces, little gifts of beauty, and I'm taking notes.

And I realize that the very act of writing down what I'm seeing and hearing is an act of recognizing the holy in the ordinary, of calling attention to it, of saying, *Look! This is worth noticing, and remembering, and paying attention to!* As I write the words *bee* and *birdsong*, I'm not feeling joy. I'm not even feeling particularly celebratory.

But Margie said that how I feel matters less than what I do, so perhaps simply noticing the bee and the birdsong means I am living celebration—living joy, even—more often than I think, certainly more often than I feel. A girl can hope anyway. And really, that's what I need to get me through these next 33 weeks: hope.

Funny. We're just a month into Ordinary Time, but I'm living in Advent, waiting and hoping; in Hebrew, I just remembered, they're the same thing: *Wait for the Lord. Hope in the Lord.*

I'm trying.

love covers

It's our tenth anniversary today. I sit at the dining table, sipping tea and flipping through our wedding album when I see the photo of Doug and me as we stand on either side of the reader board in front of our church. In the photo Doug is laughing, and I'm half-laughing. But at the time, I didn't think it was funny. Only my mouth was laughing. In my heart, I was afraid.

Between Doug and me in that photo is the church reader board. Emblazoned across the top of the board are the words "Love Covers A Multitude of Sins." Underneath that is a pink construction paper heart and the words, "Congratulations Kimberlee and Doug!"

Doug thought it was hilarious, the kind of blooper you'd read about after the end of an article in *Reader's Digest*.

I did not.

I thought it was intentional. But I was pretty good at pretending I was okay even when I was not, and I wasn't about to let on that it scared the crap out of me that someone knew all my smiling was a cover-up, a lie, so I plastered a jaunty smile on my face and posed with my laughing soon-to-be husband for a photo next to the reader board.

Today, I look at that scared smiling girl in the photo, and I want to give her a big hug. I want to tell her, "You aren't as screwed up as you think you are." I want to say, "Relax. It was an innocent *faux pas*. No one was sending you a secret threat message."

But it wouldn't have mattered. That girl was habituated to see herself through the critical eyes of the men at the Belvedere Tennis Club. As

Doug said to me during that first year we were married, "You won't believe the nice things people actually say about you, but you're more than willing to believe all sorts of mean things nobody ever said."

But somebody did say those mean things. Me. And they were echoed and magnified by the little chorus of critical voices I carried around in my head and projected onto almost everyone I met. The words on the reader board seemed to corroborate the voices in my head—on my wedding day, I didn't see the "love covers;" I only saw the "multitude of sin."

As I sit here looking at this young girl and the young man she's about to marry and the words on the reader board between them, I realize that however innocent a *faux pas* those words on the reader board were, they were also prophetic. Love really does cover a multitude of sins. Ten years of living with my husband, of living in the circle of his love for me, of slowly coming to see myself through his loving eyes instead of my own critical ones is slowly transforming me.

Oh, the tennis club men and their nasty wives are still around, for sure, but thank God, I don't listen to them quite as much these days. I'm more likely to own up to mistakes instead of hiding them or verbally flagellating myself for them. I sometimes laugh when I mess up instead of freaking out that someone is going to find out and I'll become a pariah. And I'm way more likely to tell the truth about who I am than hide behind a fake smile or a misrepresentation or even an outright lie. It's a process, of course, and oh Lord, I still have a long way to go on this journey into love and trust.

On this day, exactly ten years after he promised to love and cherish me till death do us part, I am so so so grateful to Doug for living that promise; for loving me faithfully, even when I am unlovable; for walking with me these ten years, and especially these past weeks when my belly extends in pretty much every direction and I feel ugly and weary and weepy and useless; for holding my hand and covering me with his love when I am scared and insecure; for helping me laugh at myself when I fall down or my inner ugliness gets the best of me; and for expecting me to be better than I am because that's how he sees me.

I sip my tea and think of the words of the fox in *The Little Prince*, the first book Doug and I read together: "It is only with the heart that one can see rightly." Doug's love sees a vision, a true vision, of who I am—

and even though I am not yet that person, not fully, I am more that person than I was ten years ago. His love sees rightly, sees the possibility of me as reality. *Proleptic* is the word Bible scholars use—the now that is not-yet. And it is a not-yet that somehow reaches into the now, that transforms the now into the not-yet. This is how Doug's love covers me: by seeing rightly, by seeing my not-yet fully realized self right now, his love transforms me into more of who I am.

I read the words on the reader board again: Love covers a multitude of sins. I smile at the scared girl in the photo and run my finger along the curve of her cheek, and I think how glad I am that I'm no longer her. That girl would have died of a twin pregnancy. I grin at her and think it's a good thing she didn't have the first clue what she was in for. She'd have hightailed it to Canada and become a nun and missed out on the fun of daily chocolate shakes and a growing pair of cankles.

And I wouldn't be sitting here right now marveling at how much she's grown up, how marriage has softened her and stretched her—I smirk at my bulging belly—and helped her learn to take herself a little more lightly.

Love really does cover a multitude of sins.

itchy mama

I itch. Everywhere. We're talking keep-me-up-at-night itchy here. It started two weeks ago with the soles of my feet. Over the next few days the itching spread all over my body. I itch in places I can't scratch: between my toes, inside my ears. Even my eyeballs itch.

I want to scratch off my skin.

I also want a decent night's sleep, so when I go to my doc on Friday, I ask her if there's something I can do about the itching. She gives me a low-dose Benadryl prescription and orders some blood work. "Just to rule out a liver disorder," she says.

Being the hypochondriac I am, you'd think the words "liver disorder" would freak me out. They don't. Well, okay, they do, for about five seconds. But then I remember that I've sailed through 32 weeks of this pregnancy with no complications, despite my most active imagining of the worst, so I tell myself this will be more of the same.

Only it isn't. My blood test comes back positive. I have a rare condition called cholestasis of pregnancy. My liver is unable to effectively process all the pregnancy hormones in my body, so it's releasing bile acid into my blood, and the acid is lodging in my skin—hence the itching. The real concern, though, is that it will cross over into the babies' placentas and lodge there, causing stress on their little bodies.

As I read about cholestasis, my eyes grow wide with fear. Stillbirth is one of the possible outcomes of this condition. And fetal distress. And hemorrhaging. And preterm labor, for which I'm already at higher risk, simply because I'm carrying twins.

My first thought is, let's do a C-section and get them out of there. But at 32 weeks gestation, the dangers of prematurity are a much higher risk to the babies than the danger posed by my cholestasis. So they're staying put...for now.

With cholestasis, fetal distress can occur very quickly, so my doctor wants me monitored super closely. I now have twice weekly non-stress tests in addition to my weekly appointment with her. And I'm supposed to sit down several times a day and do kick counts—literally counting how many times the babies move in 15 minutes—to make sure they're behaving normally. If they're not, it's to the hospital I go.

On top of all this, because twin pregnancies are at a higher risk for pregnancy-induced hypertension (PIH), my doc wants to make sure I don't have elevated levels of protein in my urine, an early sign of PIH. So after my appointment with her, I traipse downstairs to the lab.

When I get there, the lab lady doesn't bother to call me to the back. "You'll need to collect your urine every time you urinate for 24 hours," she says, and then, in the lobby, in front of God, a geriatric man in a wheelchair, two middle-aged women, and a teenage boy, she gives me a big—we're talking two liter—orange jug and a small cup and a funnel. She points to the cup. "Urinate into this," she says, "and then use the funnel to transfer the urine into the jug." I just stand there, blinking at her and wishing to God the floor of the lab would open up and swallow me whole. Then she says, "Once you begin collecting urine, be sure to store the jug in the refrigerator."

"The—refrigerator?" I say.

She nods. "We won't be able to get an accurate reading of the protein levels if the urine doesn't stay cold."

Ew. I wish I hadn't asked. I schlep the jug, cup, and funnel home and put the latter on the back of the toilet and the former in the refrigerator. By the time Doug gets home, I've collected several ounces of pee. When he sees the jug sitting on the shelf next to the milk, he picks it up and says, "What's this? Orange juice?"

"My urine collection bottle."

He shoves the jug back on the shelf and shudders. "Why the heck is it in the refrigerator?" Then, "Never mind. I don't want to know."

The next day, I drop the three-quarters-full jug off at the lab on my way to my non-stress test. I am glad to wash my hands of it. Literally.

This morning, I get a call from the nurse at the OB clinic. She tells me the urine analysis came back with elevated protein levels and my doctor wants to see me stat. I manage to wait till I hang up the phone before I start to cry.

I call Doug and sob into the phone. I haven't slept well in nearly two weeks—the itching continues, despite two prescriptions and a topical drug—I've been at the hospital five of the past seven days, and I've already been through an emotional zeitgeist this week with the cholestasis crap. "I'm so scared," I tell him through my tears. PIH is nothing to mess with. "Oh Doug, what if I have it?"

He is his normal rational self. "Why don't you wait to worry till you've been to see the doctor? They'll take your blood pressure, they'll check the babies' heartbeats, and then they'll be able to say what's going on, okay?"

I nod into the phone. "Okay," I say, sniffling. I make him stay on the phone till I've stopped crying and can face Jack and Jane with a smile.

I drop them off at Carrie's, thankful for her willingness to take them in at a moment's notice, and traipse back to the hospital for the sixth day out of seven. They strap the baby monitors to my belly and a blood pressure cuff to my upper arm and leave me to lie there for an hour and a half. I listen to the babies' heartbeats kathunking rhythmically on the monitor. They sound great. Even I can tell they're fine. The question is, am I?

When my doc comes in, she asks me some questions, looks at my blood pressure readings, and says, "Your blood pressure's nice and low, so I'm not worried about PIH right now. But I want your blood pressure monitored each time you come in for a non-stress test. And we should keep an eye on your protein levels."

I raise my eyebrows. "An eye on my protein levels? What does that mean?"

"It means I'll order another urine test in two weeks."

I expel a breath. Great. Another day with the orange jug.

I'm grateful that, for now at least, it appears I don't have PIH. Truly I am. But really, between the itching and the cankles, the watermelon, the rickety creaking when I waddle about, and the orange jug, this pregnancy is getting out of hand.

grace notes, july 2

Friends who watch my children while I'm at the hospital: Carrie had them for seven hours on Tuesday, God bless her, and Laura watched them yesterday afternoon when I found out I needed to schlep back up to the hospital again.

Cool weather. (I'm probably the only person in Seattle rejoicing that this was the rainiest June on record.)

Princess parking right in front of the hospital when I was at the end of my rope on Wednesday.

And while I was there, Susan watched my kids, cleaned my house, and made dinner.

A fabulous homemade lasagne delivered to our door yesterday—the day this week when I most needed it.

I don't have PIH. Thank you, Jesus.

Doug's rock-solid rationality. He always waits to worry. And even then he usually doesn't.

The babies are healthy. Much as I complain about the discomforts of this pregnancy—and they are legion—I am crazy grateful these boys are growing well.

revenge of the baby hugger

Doug comes into the bedroom while I'm dressing. I've got on my undies, a camisole, and the girdle part of my baby hugger. He laughs out loud. "I'm going to miss this," he says.

"Miss what?" I fasten one end of the velcro-and-elastic suspenders under my belly. "Miss mocking me?"

"That too."

"Very funny." I pull the suspenders around my back, crossing them over my shoulders.

When I went to the OB yesterday, they weighed me, as they always do. I'd gained eight pounds in two weeks. And my belly had turned from a 35-centimeter watermelon to a 40-centimeter beach ball. Well, it would be a beach ball, if beach balls were filled with lead.

I'd told Doug all week that I could swear I felt the babies growing. Turns out I wasn't making that up. I really was feeling them grow. A lot. Which is of course good for them—and horrible for my bladder.

The baby hugger helps...some. But it's only meant to hold up pregnant women's bellies until said women actually have their baby, which most women do by the time they measure 40 centimeters. I, on the other hand, still have at least two more weeks in which the babies—and my belly—can grow.

I don't think the baby hugger's up for it. I'm not sure I'm up for it. But I don't have a choice. The days march inexorably forward, and the only way out of this pregnancy is labor, delivery, and postpartum sleep-deprivation, which I am dreading, dreading, dreading. I shove the thought aside and make a sour face at Doug. I pull the baby hugger's suspenders over my shoulders and down to my belly. It's a bit of a stretch, even for the elastic. When I fasten the suspenders to the girdle, the velcro doesn't hold. The suspenders fly up and hit me in the face.

Doug laughs again. "Yep," he says, "I am definitely going to miss this."

queen bee

On Friday afternoon, at my non-stress test, the contraction monitor picks up a bunch of low-grade contractions that I can't even feel. Since they're a couple minutes apart, my nurse tells me, "Take it easy for the next few days, okay? Stay off your feet." This means no errands, no chores, no cooking, no cleaning.

I leave the hospital with a big grin on my face. *Glorious,* I think. *I can lie in bed and read and write and look at magazines.*

And Saturday *is* glorious. Doug, Jack, and Jane are on the church camping trip, so I have the house to myself. I laze in bed till ten, finish a book, start another, get up long enough to make myself two eggs, a piece of toast, and a cup of tea, and then go eat them in bed. I catch up on my blog reading, watch two episodes of *Lark Rise to Candleford,* and write a half dozen blog posts for after the babies are born when I'll be too sleep-deprived and hormone-ridden to string a coherent sentence together.

By the end of the day, though, I'm feeling a little tired of being in bed. I turn out the light at 9:30 and try to sleep. What a joke. Sleep has been elusive for over a month. I have to sleep sitting up because the watermelon is so heavy I can't breathe on my back, or even my side. Plus, the babies like to wake up right around the time I want to fall asleep, and then they breakdance on my bladder. Or kickbox. Whatever. It's unpleasant—and antithetical to a sleep environment.

On Sunday morning, after a weary night of dozing and waking, I feel so stir-crazy that at six, I'm ready to call it a night and get up. I decide I don't care what the nurse said. I'm going to church. And the first service at that. When left to my own devices, I never go to the first service. It requires getting up and getting ready by 8:30, and I'd rather lie in bed and read or journal. But I spent all of yesterday lying in bed and reading and journaling, and I am sick to death of being in bed. So up I get, and gladly.

Church kills a good three hours of my day, and I'm very good about sitting through the whole service, not even standing to sing or when Jim reads the Gospel passage. When I get home, I am a very good girl: I lie down for the rest of the day.

But probably, I shouldn't have gone to church: on Monday I start feeling contractions every seven minutes or so and spend two hours in triage being monitored, at which point the OB decides I'm not in labor and sends me home. Hallelujah!

On Tuesday, when I go in for my non-stress test, my contractions are coming three to seven minutes apart and Baby A (that's what they call the presenting baby, the one who will be born first) has descended into my birth canal. My nurse admits me to the L&D floor, and the nurses there hook me up to all the monitors all over again.

I call Carrie to ask if she can keep Jack and Jane through dinner. "I'll have Doug bus up to your house after work," I tell her. "Is there any way you or Rick could take him and the kids home?"

"You know what," she says, "I'll just keep them overnight, okay? Then Doug can come be with you. You sound like you could use some company."

Tears spill down my cheeks. "Thank you, friend."

I call my mom next and cry into the phone. "Can you come now? Please? I can't do this." I need another adult at home to watch Jack and Jane. My chest aches with missing them. Two nights in a row Doug and I haven't been home for dinner or stories or bedtime, and once these babies are born, their world is really going to turn upside down, and I am scared and sad for them. Oh God, why does it have to hurt so much?

Mama says, "I'll talk to your dad, but we'll make it work. We'll be there Saturday or Sunday."

I hang up the phone and cry harder. I am so scared. I start shaking uncontrollably. When the nurse comes in, she says, "Oh honey," and gets me a blanket out of the warmer. "It's just nerves," she reassures me. "Too much adrenaline."

I lie under that warm blanket and listen to the babies' heartbeats on the monitor and slowly start to relax. After three hours of staring out the window at the trees and power lines and shifting cloud shapes, Doug shows up. "I brought dinner," he says and sets down a paper take-out dish of fish and chips and a Caesar salad from the Coastal Kitchen. I don't want to eat, but I know I need to, so I do.

At nine, my contractions have slowed down to about ten minutes apart and my cervix has stabilized. The OB decides I'm not in active la-bor—yet—and says I can go home. But I have to come back tomorrow afternoon for another cervical exam. I am glad the babies are staying put for now, but I am sick of driving to the hospital nearly every day for some new drama that turns out to be nothing.

As I leave the hospital, the discharge nurse looks at me and says, "You stay off your feet, you hear? Doctor's orders." I smile and nod, but inside I am sticking out my tongue at her.

A week later, and I am sick of my bed. But I am being good. I am lying in bed pretty much all day, playing Polly Pockets with Jane (my belly is the mountain where the dragon lives), Legos with Jack, and reading *Little House on the Prairie* to both of them. At this rate, we'll finish the whole series before these babies are born.

In the week that I've been lying here, my mother-in-law and five friends have come to clean my house, watch my kids, cook my meals, do my dishes and laundry, and keep me company; and my mom and dad drove up from Cali to stay with us in case I have another false alarm or actually go into labor for real. I am grateful beyond words. I am also heartily sick of being waited on hand-and-foot, like some engorged and pulsating queen bee, who lies around gestating while her drones do all the work. It's humbling, to say the least. Sometimes it feels humiliating.

Last night, Carrie and Rick hosted a going away party for Jane's godfather, John, and his wife, Tara, who are moving to California in two weeks. The whole evening, I sat in a reclining chair with my feet up while my friends graciously brought me food and drink, made sure my kids were fed, and kept an eye on them while they played in the yard and the house. I felt very loved and cared for. I also felt like a total energy-sucking schmuck. After all, it wasn't my party.

I am sure there is a lesson for me in all this, probably several lessons, about taking care of myself and letting others help me and the dangers of an overly developed Protestant work ethic. Things like that. But honestly? I'm too tired to really ponder them.

So I don't. Instead, I heft myself into a more comfortable position and take another nap.

the things I'm looking forward to

At Vacation Bible Camp yesterday, after I dropped off Jack and Jane and was walking back to my car, I met a woman pushing her three-month-old baby in her stroller. "How far along are you?" she asked.

"Thirty-five weeks," I said, then added, almost apologetically, "I'm having twins."

"Twins! But you're so tiny! I think I was bigger than you, and I just had one!"

Yes, my frame is small, but my belly is the size of a woman who's 44 weeks pregnant. I smiled sweetly, but I wanted to smack her and say, "Like hell you were this big." Clearly the sleep-deprivation is already affecting my judgment. She meant that as a compliment, I'm sure, and here I went and felt insulted.

This afternoon, when Tiffany calls to check in on me, she tells me, "After seeing you at your shower on Sunday, I told my mom you're almost wider than you are tall!"

I tell her about the woman who said I was "so tiny" and how affronted I'd been, how I wanted to sock her in her flat stomach.

Tiffany laughs and says, "Well, if it's any consolation, I think you're huge. I think you've got the biggest pregnant belly I've ever seen."

"Thank you!" I feel mollified and gratified. I also feel enormous and very, very uncomfortable. In fact, despite having done the whole newborn thing twice before, I confess I am actually hoping for an early delivery. Tomorrow sounds about right. Yes, I know the first few weeks are going to be brutal beyond words, and the first few months won't be a whole lot better, and that I'm probably going to be a nervous wreck the way I was with Jack and, to a lesser extent, Jane. But I'm so uncomfortable and heavy and sleep-deprived and wrecked already that the postpartum period seems to offer glimmers of freedom. Among the things I'm looking forward to:

Not having this 55-pound beach ball protruding from my abdomen.

Sleeping on my back. Oh, I can hardly wait.

Not having pain in my sacrum every time I change position.

No more itching!

Being able to walk instead of waddle.

Being able to see my feet when I'm standing on them.

Hot, hot, hot showers.

Wearing clothes that fit. (I've outgrown all my pregnancy clothes because, really, who is ever 10 months pregnant?)

Calling the twins by real names instead of "Baby A" and "Baby B" (though Doug gets around this by calling them Brendan and Brandon or Sean and Shawn).

Seeing their faces for the first time.

Holding them skin-to-skin.

Being able to let *other* people hold them.

Watching Jack and Jane grow into their roles as older siblings.

And the thing I'm most looking forward to: simply not being pregnant anymore. Oh what a blessed relief that will be.

Of course, I may see all this a whole lot differently when I'm six days postpartum, bleary-eyed, even more sleep-deprived than I am now, and dealing with raging hormones and bleeding nipples. Then pregnancy might not look so bad after all.

Ordinary Time
birth
(july/august)

Come to me, all who labor and are heavy laden.

—Jesus, *The Gospel of Matthew*

day 1: "uh, doctor, there's a baby"

On my way home from my non-stress test Thursday afternoon, I go into labor. I tell myself it's just more of the false alarm contractions I've been having for the past two weeks, and I keep heading home. But a half hour after I get home, I call the hospital and tell the nurse my contractions are five minutes apart and I can't talk through them. She says to come back to the hospital. So I call Doug and ask him to come home from work. He bikes home in record time, in near record heat, changes out of his bike clothes, finishes packing our hospital bag, and we head to the hospital.

At 10:30 that night, I decide it's time for the epidural. I did the whole natural childbirth thing with Jane and decided almost the moment we learned there were twins inside me that I was opting for painkiller this time around. After the epidural line is in place and dripping painkiller into my spinal fluid, the nurse turns down the lights and says, "Try to sleep."

Yeah, right. I have a blood pressure cuff, an IV, two baby monitors, a contraction monitor, a catheter, and the epidural line attached to my body. I can't feel my legs, feet, or belly, and to move even the slightest little bit requires the help of both Doug and the nurse. I have never felt quite so much like a beached whale. Try to sleep, indeed.

The epidural, unfortunately, stops my labor cold, so when the OB—a woman I've never met before—comes in this morning at five, she breaks Baby A's bag of waters to try to get things moving again. This doesn't help me progress any, so around seven, she suggests starting a pitocin drip.

My eyes go big. Enough of my epidural has worn off that I'm feeling very strong contractions, and all I can do is breathe through them—no dice on finding a more comfortable position, not with all these tubes and monitors attached to my body—and pitocin makes your contractions even stronger. I timidly say, "Before we do the pitocin, can I get more pain relief?"

My nurse assures me that she won't start the pitocin till I'm comfortable, and she sends for the anesthesiologist, who shows up at 7:45 and gives me a bolus of epidural, which is basically as much in a minute as I'd been getting in an hour. Within five minutes, I can no longer feel my contractions.

Meanwhile, it's been shift change, and my OB is on duty. I smile with relief when she comes into the room with the ultrasound machine. "We just need to make sure the babies are still head down," she says, "so we know it's okay to attempt a vaginal birth." She finds Baby A's head, then Baby B's head, both down.

My nurse keeps moving one of the baby monitors around on my belly. She says, "I can't find Baby A's heartbeat. Can you check his position again?"

The OB runs the ultrasound wand up and down my belly, and side to side over my pubic bone, but she can't find his head. "He was just here," she says.

The nurse pulls back the blanket that covers me. "Uh, doctor," she says. "There's a baby."

Doug, who is standing by my head, holding my hand, looks down toward my feet. His eyes fill with tears, and a huge smile lights his face. "Kimberlee, there's a baby!"

Baby A is lying in the bed.

"How can there be a baby?" I say. "I didn't even push."

Laughing, my OB pushes the call button. "We need a baby nurse, stat."

My nurse is laughing. The intern attending my birth is laughing. Doug is laughing and crying. I am still confused. Then someone picks Baby A up and lays him on my chest, and I start laughing and crying, too.

Suddenly the room is full of people: the neonatal nurses, the resi-
dent, the pediatrician, a respiratory therapist, and a couple of midwives.
Everyone is laughing.

My OB checks Baby B's position with the ultrasound. He's still head
down. After five of the weakest pushes in the history of childbirth (I'm
still highly doped up on that bolus of epidural), Baby B is born to the
sound of happy conversation and laughter.

I get to hold both boys on my chest for about a minute before they're
whisked off to the special care nursery upstairs, Doug following the
nurses out of the room and down the hall to the elevator.

Later, Doug will come back downstairs and tell me he thinks we
should name Baby A Luke and Baby B Ben. Later still, my nurse will
wheel me upstairs so I can see them for myself and stroke their soft,
wrinkled skin and decide that Doug is right about their names.

For now, I lie alone in the hospital room, scribbling their birth story
in my journal and rejoicing that all those burgers and milkshakes paid
off: "Baby A weighs 5½ pounds, and Baby B weighs 6½ pounds. That's
decent for a full-term singleton, and they're near-term twins. Color me
proud of myself."

I have no way of knowing that tomorrow morning, Ben will go into
acute respiratory distress, that both his lungs will collapse, that it will
take three scary hours of doctors and nurses shouting above the strident
beeping of the machines that will be hooked up to his tiny body before
he is stabilized enough to be ambulanced to Children's Hospital. I
have no way of knowing that his left lung will collapse again during
the ambulance ride and the doctors at Children's will have to perform
another emergency surgery when he arrives, or that he will remain in
critical condition for four days, his lungs so fragile they'll keep tearing
and collapsing from the weight of the air seeping into his chest cavity.
I have no way of knowing that it will be eight long days before I get to
hold him again.

I have no way of knowing that during those scary days I will look
back and hope that his first memory of life outside the womb gave him
something beautiful to think and dream about. I have no way of knowing how it will sustain me, this remembering that the first sound he ever
heard was joy.

day 2: rescue at the last hour

When Doug and I arrive at Children's Hospital three hours after Ben arrived by ambulance, the NICU team is inserting yet another shunt into his chest to siphon air out: his lungs keep tearing, which allows air to leak into his chest cavity; the air then presses on his lungs, causing them to collapse.

When Ben is stabilized, the neonatologist comes out to where Doug and I are waiting in a little alcove off the main hallway to the NICU. She takes us across the hall to a little windowless room. Once Doug is seated (I'm already seated—in a wheelchair, as I can't yet walk), she says gently, "If Ben doesn't show signs of improvement in the next few hours, or if his lungs tear again, we're going to have to take a different approach to his care."

I reach over and grab hold of Doug's hand.

"We're not to this point yet," she says, "but I want to tell you what we'll recommend if Ben doesn't remain stable. It's called ECMO—that stands for Extra-Corporeal Membrane Oxygenation. Basically it's a lung bypass machine which pumps all his blood out of his body, removes the carbon dioxide, re-oxygenates it, and pumps it back into him. The benefits of this option are that it will give Ben's lungs a chance to heal, without the constant movement of the ventilator. But there are risks."

As she lists the risks—she says things like "blood clots" and "bleeding in the brain"; she says "hemorrhages"—I feel the blood drain out of my face.

"I'm not making this recommendation yet," she says, "but I want you to think about it, because it's likely that we'll have to go this route."

When she leaves, I call my mom and tell her what's going on. "Please don't tell the kids," I say. "I don't want them to worry. Just tell them Ben is very sick and ask them to pray, okay?"

Then I call Susan. This morning, she had sat beside me at Group Health while I held Luke and listened to the doctors and nurses shouting and the machines beeping, and she had prayed for Ben, my son, her godson.

"Kimberlee," she says after I tell her about the scary lung machine, "when you left Group Health this afternoon, I picked up your Bible and I was reading in Isaiah, and God directed me to this verse: *Those who hope in the Lord will renew their strength. They will rise on wings like eagles. They will run and not grow weary. They will walk and not be faint.*

"And I knew that he's going to be okay. He's going to live, Kimberlee. He's going to run and leap and *breathe*!"

I weep into the phone. I want to believe her. I tell her, "If Ben lives, I want you to read those words at his baptism, okay?"

"He's going to live, Kimberlee. I know it."

I don't. I am so afraid she will be reading those words at his funeral. *Blood clots. Bleeding in the brain. Hemorrhages.* The list of risks circles in my mind, over and over. *Oh God, please don't let him need ECMO. Please let him live.*

I call Jim and leave a message on his voicemail at the church. He calls back about 20 minutes later. "May I tell the congregation tomorrow?" he asks. "I know they'd love to pray for Ben."

"Yes," I say. "Yes. Please tell them. Please pray. Please pray he won't need this scary lung machine."

"I am. We all will be."

As I hang up, John and Tara walk into the waiting room. "I know you said not to come," John says to Doug, "but we were so close, we had to stop by."

They sit down across from us. I can't believe they're here. They're moving to California tomorrow. They have a going away dinner tonight.

Tara shrugs. "It doesn't start for 45 minutes. We'll hang out with you till then."

I want to weep. "Thank you." My voice is thick with tears.

A kind-looking man comes over to us and introduces himself. He's the night-shift doctor. He pulls a red cloth-covered chair up beside my wheelchair and says he's been talking with the day-shift doctor, "and we both agree that it's time to move to ECMO. Ben's lungs are simply too fragile to handle the oscillating ventilator we have him on."

I start to shake. The doctor leaves for a moment and brings me back a blanket. He places his hand on my arm. His voice is soft and reassuring. "I know it sounds scary, but I think ECMO is Ben's best chance at life."

I nod. He leaves to get the consent form Doug and I must sign, the form that lists the blood clots and bleeding in the brain and hemorrhages and says we understand these risks and are choosing to proceed with the treatment anyway.

John says, "Why don't we pray?"

I cling to Doug's hand while John prays for Ben, for us, for Luke, and for the name of Jesus to be glorified in this situation.

I sit there and all I can manage is, *Please please please. Please let Ben live. Please don't let him get a blood clot. Please keep him from bleeding in his brain. Please don't let him hemorrhage. Please.*

Tara prays, too, "for comfort for these dear friends, for strength, and courage, and wisdom."

After John says, "Amen," he looks at us. "I'm so sorry. We have to go."

I nod. "It's okay. I'm just so grateful you came. I'm so glad you were here when the doctor told us—" I break off. I can't say it. I wanted God to stop it, and He didn't. I paste a smile on my face. "Thank you. For coming. For praying."

"We'll keep praying," Tara says as she gives me a hug. And I know she will.

They head down the hall, and I watch them till they turn the corner. I'm still shaking, despite the blanket draped over my shoulders. Doug says, "When was the last time you ate?"

I shrug. "I don't know. Lunch, maybe?"

"I'm going to get you some food."

So I sit alone in the waiting room, shivering and desperately wanting to see my son. *Blood clots. Bleeding in the brain. Hemorrhages. Please*

God. Please no. Please let him be okay.

Doug is still gone when the doctor comes back.

He sits beside me and says, "You see I don't have the consent form."

I look at his hands. They're empty.

"In the past 20 minutes Ben's shown signs of wanting to get better. I'd like to wait a few hours to see if he continues in this direction. We have a four-hour window to use the ECMO machine—it's in his room and primed with donated blood—so we can start it up as soon as we need to, but for now, I think we should wait and see if he continues to improve without it."

I blink away tears. *Thank you, Jesus. Thank you, Jesus. Thank you, Jesus.* "Thank you," I say to the doctor.

"When your husband gets back, why don't you come in and see Ben?"

When Doug returns, after we eat the food he brings, he wheels me into the NICU, past rooms full of sick kids hooked up to all kinds of machines. He pushes the wheelchair into Ben's room at the end of the hall.

The ECMO machine looks like an octopus, tubes filled with blood wreathing around it. Ben lies beside the machine, his little body naked except for a diaper, tubes stuck between his ribs, in his arms, in his belly button. His face is mostly covered with a ventilator mask. I lean over him and kiss his forehead, hold his tiny hand in mine. Doug strokes his little forehead; his hands are bigger than Ben's whole head.

I whisper Susan's passage from Isaiah into his ear. "Ben, may you rise on wings like eagles, may you run and not grow weary, may you walk and not be faint." Then, for good measure, I add, "And I expect you to do those things here on this green earth, baby boy. Here, where I can watch you."

Thank you, thank you, thank you, that he's stabilized. Please, oh please, let him live.

day 4: finding nemo

The new shape of my life is a triangle.

Each morning, we drive from home to Children's to see Ben and go to rounds, where we hear about any issues he's facing and what the day's plan for him is. Then we drive from Children's to Group Health for some skin-to-skin cuddling with Luke, who is stuck in the nursery there until he figures out how to eat and breathe at the same time. And finally we drive from Group Health to home to hang out with Jack and Jane for a bit before we drive the triangle all over again, this time with the older kids in tow. Back home again, we eat dinner. Then I hook my breasts up to the hospital breastpump we're renting, and sit for ten minutes hoping all this suction will convince my breasts to make milk. After I wash the pump parts, I fall into bed, only to wake up four hours later to breastpump again. And then again in the morning before we go to rounds.

After just two days of this, I am exhausted.

When my sister calls on Monday afternoon to find out what's going on, I tell her I'm feeling anxious. "Ben desatted again today, so they had to bump his oxygen back up."

"Desatted? What kind of word is that?"

"It means that his blood isn't getting enough oxygen; it's leaking out through those holes in his lungs, so they have to increase the amount of oxygen they're pumping into him."

He'd been at or very close to 100% oxygen for the first two days, but they were finally able to lower it today. "He was all the way down to 45%," I tell Jen, "but when he desatted this afternoon, they had to bump him back up to 65%. The good news is that it's not 100%. At 65%, they at least have somewhere to go; if he desatted when he was up at 100%, there was nowhere they could go."

I am so grateful that he hasn't needed the ECMO machine, so grateful that he's doing better than he has been. And I am so anxious that he regressed. The doctor said today that he is not doing as well as she would like, that ECMO is still a possibility.

"Do they know why this is happening?" Jen asks. "I mean, why his lungs keep tearing?"

I shake my head. "No one seems to be able to explain why he's getting the nemothoraces," I tell her.

Doug, who's driving, says, "Pnuemothoraces."

"What?" I say.

"They're *pneumo*thoraces."

"Oh," I say. "Duh." I start laughing into the phone. "Uh, Jen, they're *pneumo*thoraces, like in pneumonia; not *nemo*thoraces, like in *Finding Nemo*. I've been saying that word wrong for three days now."

She laughs with me. "You know how happy it makes me that you messed that up?"

"You know how happy it makes me to be laughing right now?"

"Yes," she says, "I think I do."

day 7: hard

Tonight I am taking a shower. I should be sleeping, but I can't remember the last time I was clean. I'm a week postpartum, still bleeding, and a total mess. The nurses at Group Health keep telling me I should be taking two baths a day. *Yeah right*, I think as I step under the shower spray. I'll do that just as soon as Doug installs a bathtub in the sofamobile so I can bathe while we're driving.

As I'm gingerly washing my sore breasts, I discover some swelling in my right armpit and three hard little lumps. It's 11 p.m., I've been up since six a.m., and I am tired, weary, and not thinking clearly, so of course in my imminently rational state, I immediately diagnose myself with breast cancer and start imagining my funeral—all the sad head-shaking of people from church who don't know me very well and all the kind things the people who do know me will say and how Doug will get remarried and a stranger will raise my children—and a whole-body wave of panic sweeps through me, and I feel sick. I actually have to lean against the shower wall to keep myself from falling over. I tell myself I'm just tired and it's making me irrational, but I'm too tired and too irrational to believe myself. I fall into bed fighting fear, no longer for Ben, who is improving in leaps and bounds, but for me.

When my alarm goes off at 3 a.m. so I can get up and pump, I wake with anxiety lying like a rock on my chest. I tell myself I'm worried about Ben, so I call the hospital to check on him. He's fine, the nurse assures me; he's down to 42% oxygen in his ventilator. I nod, relieved that I wasn't having a premonition of bad things to come, but the fear doesn't dissipate.

In the morning, I pump again, and those three lumps are still there. I'm concerned, but not panicking, and I breathe a prayer of thanks for that grace.

While Doug drives to Children's, I sit in the passenger seat and return phone calls, trying to keep my dad and sister and various friends apprised of what's going on with Ben.

"He got taken off the oscillating ventilator yesterday," I tell my dad. "He's just on a regular ventilator now."

"So he's doing better?" Papa says.

"Yes. Much better."

After rounds and a visit with Ben, we head over to see Luke, and I call my sister to give her an update. "They're going to extubate Ben later today!" I tell her when she answers the phone.

"What the heck does that mean?" she asks.

I laugh. "It means they're going to take out the ventilator apparatus that's in his mouth and nose. He'll be breathing on his own. We'll be able to see his face. We might even get to hold him!"

Jen is silent a moment. "I forget," she says, "that you haven't been able to even hold him. I feel so removed from everything down here."

"You'll get to hold him when you get here," I say. "He'll probably be back at Group Health by the time you come."

"Does it strike you as wild that he's so much better so quickly?"

"Yes. Even the doctors and nurses are amazed." I want to say I think it's because so many people are praying for Ben. I want to say God is fighting hard for Ben. But Jen doesn't believe in God, and I'm not sure how to say this, given that other people are praying for their children and God isn't healing them. I believe He's fighting for those kids, too, so why isn't He winning? It's a mystery I completely don't understand, so I don't say anything about God or prayer or mystery. I just tell Jen I'm glad she's coming, that I can't wait to see her.

***

While I'm breastfeeding Luke, the midwife stops by the nursery to see how he's doing, and I ask her about the swelling and the lumps. She asks if they showed up after my milk came in.

"Yes," I say. "I just noticed it last night."

She smiles and squeezes my shoulder. "Don't worry about it. It's just a couple of clogged ducts. Put hot compresses on them after you breast-feed or pump."

I feel like a total dork, but I've been running on adrenaline all week, I'm hardly sleeping, and I'm finally crashing.

In the afternoon, one of the doctors at Children's extubates Ben. For the rest of the day his CO_2 levels are erratic; there is air in his left lung cavity on his four p.m. X-ray; and his breathing remains rapid, shallow, and labored. When I call the nurse just before pumping and bed, she tells me Ben's CO_2 levels are back up to 57—they were at 49 this after-noon. If the CO_2 gets up to 60, she says, they'll have to reintubate him.

As I sit here in the dark living room with these two stupid breast pump flanges sucking milk out of my nipples, all I can think is, *Oh God, he's going back to last Saturday,* and I weep.

Mama sits on the sofa across from me. "You need to stay strong, sweetie," she says. "You need to be positive. Ben is going to be fine."

I cry harder. We don't know that. We just don't, and saying it won't make it true, and I'm superstitious enough to believe that we tempt fate when we make such declarations. But I can't tell Mama this because she doesn't believe in fate, and she'd just tell me I'm not supposed to, either, and I know this, but I haven't slept well in I don't know how many months, and I'm just. not. rational.

"Sweetie," Mama says, "Be strong. The strength of the Lord is your might."

Tears stream down my face, and I can't even wipe them away because I have to hold on to these idiotic pump flanges so they don't fall off my breasts and dump my precious milk all over my lap. Tears drip off my chin.

"You can do all things through Christ who gives you strength," Mama says. "You need to be strong, sweetie. Your kids need you to be strong."

Doug opens the door to our bedroom and steps into the living room. "You know, Carol," he says softly, "I think what Kimberlee needs right now is just for you to acknowledge that this is hard."

God bless that man.

"Oh…" Mama's voice trails off. She reaches over and pats my knee.

We sit here, her hand on my knee, the only sound the wheezing of the breast pump and my quiet tears, which slowly run dry as my mom abides with me in my sadness and fear.

day 10: druggies

When we get to Children's at 8:30 for rounds, Ben's nurse tells us he'll be leaving at nine to go back to Group Health. "The transport team is on their way down," she says. "Why don't you give him a kiss and then head over to Group Health, so you can be there when he arrives?"

I am shocked. The nurses and doctors have been telling us all week to expect him to be here for three weeks. I find Maggie, one of the doctors, and ask her if she's sure this is a good idea. She smiles at me. "Kimberlee, we'd never let him leave if we didn't believe he was ready. He's ready. He's doing great." I must look as worried as I feel because she squeezes my arm and says again, "He's going to be fine."

I nod and head back to Ben's room to kiss him. Then Doug and I drive over to the Group Health nursery to welcome him. It's so fun to see both babies together, sharing a crib, their little matching caps all that's visible above their blankets. I give Doug a big hug. Both of us are a little weepy.

An hour after Ben gets settled in, I start feeling achy and getting chills.

Kaci, one of the nurses, is giving Luke his daily shot of liquid caffeine in his breast milk; the caffeine is supposed to help organize his little brain, help him be able to prioritize breathing over eating when he has to choose. I tell her I'm not feeling well.

She looks me over. "You need to go see a doctor. I think you have mastitis."

"I've never had mastitis," I protest. "Not with either Jack or Jane, and I breastfed both of them for 16 months."

Kaci turns to Doug. "Take her downstairs and get her an appointment. She needs to be on antibiotics stat."

Doug and I go downstairs and learn that one of the doctors has an opening in two hours. She diagnoses me with mastitis and writes me a prescription, which Doug picks up.

That night I feel horrible. It's ninety degrees in the house, and I'm shivering under a down blanket. Every muscle in my body aches. And my poor tender nursing breasts feel like they've been run over by a Mack truck and then set on fire.

I am refusing to feel sorry for myself, even though I really, really want to. I keep reciting a litany of reasons to be thankful. Ben's recovery is on the top of the list. Antibiotics are a close second.

***

I stay home the next day while Doug and Mama take turns visiting the twins. I hate to do it, but when I call the hospital Kaci says, "Don't come. I won't let you in if you do. You need rest, Miss Mama. Stay home tomorrow, too."

I miss my babies. I want to hold them. I hold Jack and Jane instead. They cuddle up in bed with me. I read to them when my head doesn't hurt too much. And I sleep. And pump.

Of course.

***

To make up for staying home the day after my mastitis diagnosis, I make two treks to the hospital today, and it about does me in. My mom and I leave at 7:45 and get home around noon. After lunch, I nap for an hour and then Doug and I head back to see the babies. On the way home, I am so tired I cry for fully ten minutes.

When Doug and I get home at 6:45, my mom pulls me aside. "Your kids have been waiting for you for over an hour. They went outside at 5:30 and sat right there—" she points through the window to the railroad ties in the front yard—"and waited for you. They were counting cars."

My chest aches. I can just see them sitting there waiting and waiting for us, in vain.

Mama says, "That's why I called Doug. I wanted to know what time you were going to be home."

I look at Doug. He didn't tell me my mom called.

"And you hadn't even left yet! So I called them in for dinner." She is silent a moment. "You need to stop being gone so much. They need you."

Tears form in the corners of my eyes. I look at Jack and Jane, wrestling on the living room carpet with Doug. I don't know how to have there be enough of me. How do I give each of my children enough time and attention? Not to mention Doug and my friends and my writing, which is all but nonexistent these days. And myself. My poor body has been through the ringer these past months; my soul feels fragile; my mind, fuzzy.

Lord, have mercy. How am I supposed to manage all these competing needs and desires?

The tears drop onto my cheeks. Mama sees them and gives me a hug. "Come on. You need to eat."

I follow her to the kitchen. "Sit down," she says. "I'll heat it up for you. I saved you each a plate. The woman who stopped by this afternoon brought this meal and two more for the freezer. You have an amazing community, you know."

I do know. I also don't have any idea how I'm going to manage meals once the people of my church stop feeding us, or how I'm going to manage dishes and laundry without my mom here. I already feel stretched too thin.

"Doug," Mama calls. "Come eat."

He gets himself a beer and then sits down next to me at the table. Jane pulls herself into his lap. Jack leans against my chair, his arm around my shoulders. I put my arm around his skinny waist. "I'm sorry we weren't home for dinner," I tell him.

"It's okay, Mama. You're here now."

I blink back tears and smile at him.

Doug and I hold hands, and Jane prays. "Thank you, Jesus, for this food. Thank you for the farmers who grew it and—" she looks at me "—who made it?"

I shrug. "I don't know, sweetie. Someone from church."

"—and for the person from church who made it. We pray for

Michaela and John's father and Ben. Amen. Dada?" she says in the same breath. "May I have some of your beer?"

Doug pours most of the beer into his glass, then hands her the bottle. She swigs the tablespoon left at the bottom, and I have to laugh. "Just look at us," I say. "Jane swills beer, Ben's on morphine—"

"Luke gets baby lattes!" Jack says.

I tousle his hair. "—and now thanks to mastitis, I'm on drugs, too."

Mama laughs, and Doug grins.

I wink at Jack and Jane and whisper conspiratorially, "Just don't tell anyone from CPS about our drug issues, okay, kids?"

"Okay," Jack says.

"What's CPS?" Jane says.

Mama says, "Really, Kimberlee, was that necessary?"

It wasn't. But joking with my kids makes me feel better.

day 14: grace notes (august 6)

The miracle of Ben's rapid recovery: the doctors and nurses at Children's told us to expect him to be in the NICU for a good three weeks, and he was well enough to return to Group Health (and his brother!) after just ten days. Now, at 14 days, he's been weaned off all his drugs, IV fluids, and supplemental oxygen. He's breathing on his own and now has only a feeding tube—and he's begun to practice breastfeeding.

We only have to visit one hospital now, instead of two. Glory be.

Luke's feeding tube came out this week, and he's begun actively breastfeeding. He may even be able to come home next week.

My mother, God bless her, dropped everything to come be with me. I don't know how we would have made it through the past two weeks without her.

Our community at church and Doug's colleagues have been faithfully providing meals for our family. It's such a gift to come home from the hospital and have a meal waiting for us.

The prayers of our church community and friends across the country have given Doug and me strength we didn't know we had.

Doug's steadiness, strength, and faith. I have leaned hard on him these past weeks, and he has held me.

Jane's faithful prayers for Michaela and for her baby brothers.

day 18: pumping

We spend Sunday night at the hospital, rooming in with Luke. He has no monitors, no tubes, nothing to distinguish him from any other baby who is 38-weeks gestational age. Monday morning, we bring him home.

Nice as it was to have both boys at what Doug calls the baby petting zoo (we pop in, hold them for awhile, and pop back home again while the nurses do all the hard work), I'm so glad to have Luke home. Of course, it's not all sunshine and roses. In fact, it's a horribly gray day in Seattle. In August. Which is supposed to be our nicest month of the year. Sometimes this city is seriously lame.

Anyhoo, back to Luke: though he eats three meals a day at the breast, he has to be topped off with a bottle, and his other five or six meals are strictly from a bottle. This means the shape of my life is no longer a triangle. It's a cone.

That's the shape of the flange on my breast pump.

I feed Luke, then I pump. Then I wash my pump. Then I feed Luke again. Or pump. Or both.

There's a Beautiful South song that's been in my head all day: "36D, so what? D, so what? Is that all that you've got?" On the cover of the single is a lingerie model holding a watermelon. In my book, 36D does not qualify as a watermelon. I should know. I carried around a watermelon in lieu of my waist for several months.

And I am happy to report that the watermelon has left the premises. Of course, in its place I have a couple of cantaloupes that migrated a bit north, so it's possible my belly only looks smaller in comparison. Truly, these things are bigger than they've ever been. If they keep this up, I'll be able to give Dolly Parton a run for her money. I'm only partly kidding. They really are that big. My size 36D bra is way too small.

I need to go bra shopping, desperately—because, you know, I don't have anything better to do with my time.

On Monday, I squeeze in a quick trip to Target, but alas, Target does not carry cantaloupe-sized bras. On Tuesday, on our way home from visiting Ben, Doug and I stop by Nordstrom, which is where I should have gone in the first place. Cheap outerwear is fine, but cheap bras are not, especially when you're nursing: a crummy bra can cause clogged ducts and mastitis. And mastitis is not an experience I care to repeat.

Unlike Target, Nordstrom carries all manner of random bra sizes, and they have saleswomen who know how to help you find the right one. My saleslady takes one look at my three-week-old Target nursing bra and says, "Oh, sweetie," in a tone that mixes both horror and pity. "Let's find you something that fits."

I ditch the 36D Target bra and come home with two 34H nursing bras. Yes, H. As in humongous. I'm just grateful it's not a W for watermelon, though by the time we get home, my cantaloupes are nearly the size of watermelons, and I am in pain. The second I walk in the door, I wash my hands and attach myself to the breast pump. Jack and Jane come in to tell me about their day.

"Luke pooped a big poop!" Jane announces.

"It was all over the changing pad," Jack says. "We even had to change his clothes."

They see absolutely nothing strange about this wheezing contraption I'm wearing. Or about talking to me while it's sucking milk out of my breasts.

"Look, Mama," Jack says, "you've got almost—" he leans over to look more closely at the line markings on the bottle "—almost two ounces already. Just in that one bottle!"

I smile, remembering the first time I pumped more than a few drops. Jack and Jane jumped up and down, squealing with excitement.

What can I say? We are a simple people.

Ordinary Time
zombies
(august/september)

Up from the great river's brim
Comes a cold breath; the farther bank is dim;
The heaven is black with clouds and coming rain;
High soaring faith is grown a heavy task,
And all is wrong with weary heart and brain.

—George MacDonald, *Diary of an Old Soul*

chaos

The day Ben comes home from the hospital—he's three weeks old today—we decide to move the crib from the kids' room into our bedroom. This requires that we take the crib apart because it won't fit through the bedroom door.

So here we are: the crib is in pieces; Jack and Jane are running around screaming; the babies are beyond tired and wailing like banshees; and our bed is piled with bins full of baby clothes and burp cloths and who knows what else, so there's nowhere put the babies down except on their tummy time mat, which makes them cry harder and makes me afraid Jack or Jane in their exhaustion-induced frenzy will trample them.

My mother looks fried as she holds a wailing Luke, so I can only imagine how I look. She keeps saying, "Of all the times to not have the crib."

And poor Doug is trying to simultaneously put the crib together and corral the older kids.

I sit on the sofa and breastfeed Ben to calm him down.

"Mama!" Jane runs into the living room. "Mama! I need you to brush my teeth!"

At that exact moment, Luke realizes that Ben is getting fed and he isn't, and he freaks out, wails so hard his uvula quivers.

I reorganize my nursing pillow, shove another blanket under Ben's head and a pillow under his feet. Then I get Luke latched on to my other breast. Then I brush Jane's teeth.

My mother stares. "That's impressive."

I can't help it. I low. "Mooooooo."

My mom laughs.

"Why are you mooing, Mama?" Jane asks in a garbled voice, trying to get her words past the toothbrush.

"Because I feel like a flipping cow."

Doug finally gets the crib together. While he makes bottles, my mom makes the crib and pulls all the bins off the bed and stacks them against the wall. Then each of them takes a baby from my breast and tops him off with a bottle of expressed breast milk. Meanwhile I sit on my bed and breastpump. I also read Jack and Jane their bedtime story. While breastpumping.

The next morning, while my mom makes her pot of coffee and Doug and I sip our tea, Doug says, "Man, I slept like a baby last night."

Mama looks up from her coffee. "Really?"

He nods. "Yep. I woke up every two or three hours, crying."

I nearly spit out my tea.

zombieland

Luke has a Harrison Ford smile! A half-grin that's only on one side of his face. It's just too impish and adorable.

Of course, I don't think he's impish and adorable in the middle of the night when we're giving him his fifth bottle in as many hours and he doesn't zonk out until four. Many more nights like this, and Doug and I are going to start hitting the bottle—and I'm not talking about baby bottles—or the children, neither of which is really a good option.

The boys have both been home for almost three weeks now, and I'm starting to think maybe the baby petting zoo was a better option than we thought. At least then I was only getting up once a night to breast pump. Now, Doug and I are both up and up and up.

This morning, when the boys wake up at 3:30 for the third (or is it fourth?) time and my breast pump won't work and every muscle in my body aches and my breasts feel like they're going to break off and I sort of wish they would just so they'd stop hurting, I cry with frustration and self-pity.

The grace in all this is that night passes. Day always dawns.

And when sunlight streams through our blinds, even though I still feel tired and achy, life is slightly more bearable simply because the sun is out and light drips through the windows.

Ben wakes up and starts to whimper, then wail.

My chronically chipper and cheerful husband rolls over in bed, puts the pillow over his head, and moans. "I'm beginning to crave brains."

"Me, too." I say. I crawl out of bed to go get Ben. I now understand why zombies eat brains: their own brains are so foggy and muddled from never sleeping, they need to supplement with someone else's.

"At least it's sunny again today," I say as I latch Ben onto my breast. "Sunshine helps stabilize my mercurial emotions."

I stare at the light seeping through the blinds. "Is it redundant to say *mercurial emotions?*" I ask Doug.

"For you, perhaps."

***

When I talk to my sister later in the day and tell her that we're living in zombieland out here, she says, "I'll be there Sunday. You can have my brain—because we both know I hardly use it."

I snort into the phone.

sunbreak

Doug's back at work today. I feel strangely anxious about that. After all, my mom's still here, my sister's here.

It must be the weather. Why must it be overcast the first week of September?

The babies are sleeping right now, so I've snatched these few precious moments to journal, but they'll wake soon to feed. I dread it. My nipples hurt so much I cried during Ben's 4 a.m. feeding. This sucks. Literally, it sucks—or the babies do. *Oh God, help me. Please keep me from crying. I'm tired of crying. And I really don't need more sinus congestion, okay?*

A sunbreak as I write. Light falls across my journal. My hand and my pen cast a shadow on the page. I remember what Jane told me the other day: "Sunshine is like God."

I need all of both I can get.

javier and oswald

The babies were up almost every hour all night long. Now that she's here, my sister is doing the feedings with me so Doug can sleep. She and I are running on about an hour and a half of sleep today. You'd think the babies would be tired, too, and actually sleep. But such is not the case. Jen wears Luke in the Moby, which is a really long piece of cloth that you tie around yourself in such a way that it makes a cozy cocoon for the baby while leaving your hands free to do things like brush your teeth or your hair. Jen dances around the living room, trying to get Luke to fall asleep, while I lie on the carpet with Ben.

My niece comes in from outside. "Which baby is that, Mom?" she asks.

Jen says, "This is Javier."

Atlee grins. "No, it's not! Which baby?"

Jen shrugs. "I told you. It's Javier."

Jane comes in, looking for Atlee.

"Jane! My mom says that baby's name is Javier!" Both girls giggle.

Jen rubs Luke's bald pate. "Javier with no hair," she says.

The girls giggle more. Jack comes in from the backyard. Atlee and Jane point at Luke. "Javier!" says Atlee.

"With no hair!" says Jane.

"It's the Nair," Jen says, "that makes Javier have no hair."

Jack grins.

"I climb the stair," says Jen, "holding Javier with no hair because of the Nair."

"In a chair!" Jack says.

"Right-o," Jen says. She strikes a pose and declaims in an affected accent:

"I climb the stair
in a chair
holding Javier
With No Hair
because of the Nair."

In giggles, the kids collapse onto the sofa. Jen and I laugh with them.

"Who's that, then?" Atlee asks, pointing at Ben, who is drooling onto his tummy time mat.

Jen doesn't miss a beat. "That," she says, "is Oswald. Oswald the Bald."

The kids grin. Jen continues,

"Oswald the Bald is appalled—"

She seems to be stuck, so I jump in:

"Oswald the Bald
is appalled
that Javier
With No Hair
is up there."

I point up at Luke, strapped to Jen's chest in the Moby.

For the rest of the day, Jack, Jane, and Atlee call the boys Javier and Oswald. They even make nametags and pin them to the babies' backs so Doug will know who they're talking about when he gets home.

***

After their bath this evening, both boys are wailing. Mama holds Luke, Jen is putting Ben in his sleeper, and we're all standing in my bedroom, wide-eyed and deafened.

"Are we having fun yet?" I yell above the babies' cries.

"This is hippo guano crazy!" Jen shouts back.

"We're nuts!" I yell. "We're nuts! We're crazy in our coconuts!"

But the three of us are smiling and laughing, and the boys calm down as soon as I, wincing, put them on my breast.

"Wow," Jen says. "The sound of silence."

"Thank heavens," Mama says.

Doug walks in, takes one look at me, and says, "You rock, you know that, right?"

I raise an eyebrow. "Thanks, but this isn't exactly my favorite thing."

"What isn't?" he asks.

"The double football hold here. I feel like a cow."

"Is it better if one of them is in cross cradle?"

"No. I still feel like a cow."

He cocks me a grin. "But a ninja cow."

Jen snarfs, trying to choke back a laugh.

"No," I say. "Just a cow."

Doug and Mama burst out laughing, Jen coughs and laughs, and I smile, grateful we're laughing. It beats crying any day of the week.

"Look," Jen says and points to the boys. "Javier and Oswald are holding hands."

I look down at my chest. Their tiny hands clutch each other.

"Awwww," Doug says, but his eyes are tender. We exchange a smile. I have to admit, moments like this, having twins has its compensations.

grace notes, september 10

I do not have triplets. That is the first grace of this day. And every day. The mind-numbing sleep deprivation, which I thought was horrific with just one baby, is an order of magnitude worse with two; I simply cannot imagine three.

Today's second grace is that in the midst of this hellishness I still manage to count my blessings. Well, during the day I manage to. In the middle of the night, it's a different matter.

So that's today's third grace: night always ends. Day always breaks.

I also see God's grace in so many small ways...

Laughter: in the middle of Wednesday night, Luke woke himself up with an explosive poop that I swear you could hear in the backyard. Doug and I laughed so hard I cried.

Jane hugs: yesterday afternoon, I was feeling utterly depleted—the boys ate near constantly, and I was wiped out—and Jane gave me a huge hug. It totally filled me up.

Sweet moments of motherhood: sitting in the rocking chair last night with Jack and Luke in my lap. Luke dozed on Jack's chest, my arms around them both.

My sister: she makes me laugh. She also took the 5:00 feeding this morning without waking me up: Doug and I got four uninterrupted hours of sleep. That's more than I've had in months.

My book club: Monday evening I got to hang out with six of my favorite women ever and discuss *Mansfield Park*. The fact that I managed to read *Mansfield Park* is itself cause for rejoicing. And even though this is one of my least favorite Austen novels (only *Northanger Abbey* rates lower), life doesn't get a whole lot better than good friends, a cup of tea, and a conversation about books.

A hot shower.

Ben's first smile—ever!—this morning.

Healthy children. (Thank you thank you thank you, God!)

Doug's job. Even though I hate that he's gone all day, I'm so grateful he has work.

Bouquets of phlox, hydrangea, and daisies from Jack, Jane, and Atlee. Exactly what I need here on my bedside table: beauty to behold.

Sunny days. It is so much easier to be sleep-deprived when the sun is out.

Singing hymns with my mom tonight as we rock the boys to sleep.

bed

I am sitting in bed, trying to put words to paper. Doug is zonked out on his side, the babies are zonked out between us, Jack and Jane are sitting on the foot of the bed—they want me to read to them—and I just want to be alone with my journal and my pen and my thoughts, and I think, *oh God I am never going to be alone again.*

Luke and Ben are sweet, especially when they're sleeping, and I love them, but I miss the life I had before I got pregnant. I miss teaching Jack to read and Jane to count. I miss one-on-one time with them. I miss writing. I even (almost) miss getting rejected: at least it meant I was moving forward.

I write in my journal how I wept this morning on hearing Jane's voice when she woke up—how I realized anew that this is all so fleeting, that she won't always have the sweet, piping voice of a three-year-old and that I will forget what her voice sounds like. I want to hold on to her, to Jack, to our life as it is—or rather as it was before the babies were born, before I got pregnant even. Not that I wish we didn't have the boys—hard as it is, I couldn't send them back, not now. But I do miss the sweetness, the closeness, the freedom and structure, of my life with Jack and Jane before all this—meaning my pregnancy—happened.

I write, *I am just now—just now!—realizing that life is a long journey of letting go. We embrace for a season and then we have to release those we love. How do we live with love and joy, without fear of pain, when we finally see that loss and the grief that accompanies it are the price of love, the price of any life worth living?*

Anxiety grips my chest in its icy claw. I swallow hard against it, try to loosen its grasp. I must not look back to what has been. I must not flee ahead to what might be. I must live here, now, present in and to the present. Here is a sweet girl with honey hair and dimples. Here is a goofy boy who wants to be a great swordfighter. Here is the man who loves me. Here are two healthy babies. Here is joy and beauty and love. Here is life.

All that is to come—is to come, and I can be present to that time, whatever of joy or pain it holds, only by learning now to be present to this time.

Jack hands me *Farmer Boy*. "Please, Mama?"

I look at him, his tousled hair, his hopeful grin, and I cap my pen. "How about we read on the sofa, so your dad and the boys can sleep?"

Jack and Jane hop down from the foot of the bed. I pile out after them, and we snuggle down on the couch and read.

tea and jesus

I cry as I watch my parents' car pull away from the curb and drive down
the street. I don't know how I'm going to manage without my mother.
She's been doing my dishes and laundry for two months now. She's kept
the house clean and tidy, and I just know it's all going to go to Hades
now that she's gone.

She knows it, too. Last night while she was folding towels, she
watched me wince and cringe when I latched Luke onto my breast to
feed him. She asked me, "Are you going to be okay?" She wasn't just
asking about my nipple pain.

I tried to smile. "I have to be."

She looked around the house, at the bottles drying on the dish rack,
at the piles of clothes she was folding and the pile she was pulling from.
"How are you going to manage this on your own?" It was a genuine
question, one for which I had—still have—no answer. I don't know
how. I just know I have to.

I said, "Tea and Jesus."

She laughed. "Maybe with the order reversed?"

"Maybe, but I have a feeling there's going to be a whole lot of tea
involved."

My parents' car turns the corner and disappears from sight. I wipe
the tears away and turn to watch Jack and Jane climb the hedge. Then
I go inside and do the dishes and check email, and when Jack and Jane
come in, we make grape jelly.

Yes, we do.

I am eight weeks postpartum with twins and I am making grape jelly.

If someone else had done this, I would hate her guts. What kind of supermom freak of nature makes grape jelly *ever*, let alone with infant twins?

But what else can I do? Jack and Jane spent two days picking the grapes from our grape arbor, and they begged me for two more days to make the jam. Jack especially wants to make it "because it comes from our own grapes, Mama." Apparently, that somehow makes it way cooler.

Luckily for me, it is a lousy year for grapes, at least in our yard: they only managed to pick two pounds.

Unluckily for me, when Jen was here and went on her cleaning rampage through my house, she gave away all my canning jars and lids because I knew, with four children, that I was never going to use them again.

But since we only have two pounds, I decide we don't really need to can the stuff. We can just sock it in the refrigerator as soon as it gels.

The kids and I peel the grapes. It's actually pretty fun, popping them out of their peels. Then we puree the peels with sugar and cook the puree with the peeled grapes. As we're running this concoction through the food mill to sift out the grape seeds, both babies wake up. And they're hungry.

While I sit on the sofa and lactate, Jack stirs the boiling jam till it gels. Then he pops it into the refrigerator. When I'm done nursing, Jack, Jane, and I have tea and toast with grape jelly.

I tell myself that if I can make grape jelly the day my parents leave to go home to Cali, I can do anything. And if I can't, there's always tea and Jesus.

crying

Oh. Dear. God.

The babies have been crying all morning. After an hour, I finally got Ben to sleep, only for Luke to wake him up with his incessant wailing. Luke's not hungry, he's not wet or dirty, he doesn't even want to be held. He's tired. Or insane. And he's driving me insane. I walk into the bedroom to pick him up and walk right back out again. I am afraid I am going to punch him in the head.

So I do the only reasonable thing to do: I swear. Silently, of course, so Jack and Jane can't hear me. Then I sit down and cry.

I knew this was going to be a hard week: my first full week at home with four kids and without my mom. But this morning sucks harder than I thought it would. Usually the babies nap in the a.m. for a couple hours so I can hang out with my older kids, do a load of laundry, and wash a couple dishes. Not today. Oh no. Not today.

Today Luke is crying and won't sleep, and all the rocking, breast-feeding, shushing, swaddling, and swinging in the world isn't going to help him stop wailing. I hate just letting him lie in his crib and cry, but I don't know what else to do. I have three other kids to attend to. They need to eat something. I need to eat something. I need to put in a load of laundry: we are completely out of burp cloths and baby wash cloths, even though I have about a thousand of each. Mostly I need to pray, but my brain is so addled all I can manage is, *Jesus, help. Jesus, help. Jesus, help.*

I put on the Moby and stick Luke in it, trying to be gentle and patient with this wailing baby whom I don't even like right now.

Jesus, help. Jesus, help.

"It's okay, Luke. It's okay," I say softly. Once he's secure, I rock back and forth and pat his bum. He keeps wailing, but at least he's crying on my chest, so I don't feel like a Bad Mom for letting him cry alone.

After another hour of my rocking and shushing and Luke's incessant crying, I decide I'll keep Ben, who is still asleep, the angel, but I'm going to send Luke back. He's clearly defective. I want to exchange him for the model with a mute button.

special

Ben sits in the little baby swing beside the sideboard. As I walk past him on my way to the kitchen to make a cup of tea, I'm struck again with awe that he is even alive. Who are we that our son should be spared? Should be brought back from the brink of death?

I kneel in front of the swing where he's rocking back and forth, and I tell him how much I love him, tell him how he's been set apart, saved, for a purpose. Tears gather in my eyes as I tell him how he is special.

Drool dribbles down his chin, his tongue lolls out of his mouth, and he gives me the stink eye. I laugh through my tears. He sure doesn't look all that set apart and special right now.

Unless you mean "special."

I think of the conversation, years ago, with my mom, when I told her I'd started dating someone. "His name is Doug," I'd said into the phone. "We met at church."

She asked me what he did for a living.

"He used to work at Microsoft, but he quit, so he could move into a L'Arche community."

"L'Arche?" Mama had said. "What's that?"

"It's a community for people with developmental disabilities," I explained.

"Whaaat?" Mama's voice screeched in my ear. "He's *retarded*?"

I wasn't sure if I was more offended by her un-P.C. use of the word *retarded* or her assumption that I was so desperate that I'd date someone who was.

"Oh for heaven's sake, Mama! He's a volunteer! He makes meals and takes the core members to work or the doctor. And it is so not okay to call them retarded. They're developmentally disabled." Then I'd laughed. "When you meet Doug, I'll introduce him as my 'special' friend. It takes on a whole new meaning, doesn't it?"

I look at Ben, cross-eyed and drooling. Yup, this one, he's my special son. My miracle baby. And I thank God every day that he's alive. Alive and healthy and whole. I don't deserve that kind of goodness, and yet, here it sits, right in front of me, stink-eye, drool, and all. I kiss the top of Ben's head and breathe another prayer of gratitude for his life.

needing magic

When Julianne comes over to watch the kids, she says she wants to give me a break so I can take a shower or a nap or something. I tell her I have a prescription to pick up and would she feel comfortable watching the kids while I'm gone?

Jane declares that she wants to go with me, and Luke suddenly starts wailing. I grab him out of his crib so he doesn't wake Ben and bring him back to the living room.

"It should only take a half hour or so," I say.

Julianne says it's fine with her.

But I'm feeling anxious. I can't imagine being without one or more of my children, so I take Jane and Luke with me to the pharmacy, leaving Ben asleep and Jack happily making origami birds with Julianne.

When we get there, the lobby is packed. There's only one chair, so Jane has to sit in my lap. I set Luke, who fell asleep in the car and is still strapped into his baby seat, on the floor. Jane and I read through the entirety of James Herriot's *Treasury for Children* while we wait and wait and wait for our number to be called. After each story, I look at the clock on the wall and start to panic. I managed to leave my cell phone at home, and I told Julianne I'd only be a half hour, and what if there's an emergency and she can't reach me and what if she needs to be somewhere and maybe I should just go home and come back tomorrow with all four kids. That thought is so daunting that I immediately reject it and force myself to read Jane another story to focus my thoughts on something other than my crazy-making anxiousness.

Finally, after 45 minutes, after I'm so flooded with anxiety that I think I might cry, a pharmacy worker calls my number. I carry Luke in his carseat up to the window. Jane stands beside me, the James Herriot book folded against her chest.

I tell the pharmacist I'm here to pick up my magic nipple cream. It's not called that, really, but that's what Doug and I call it. I'd used it after Jane was born, and it kept me breastfeeding when her tiny little mouth kept blistering my nipples. This stuff has some kind of mild steroid in it that promotes rapid healing of your skin. It's awesome, and I can hardly wait to start using it on my poor, blistering, bleeding nipples. You'd think after two months of breastfeeding, they'd be used to it. They're not.

The pharmacist looks up my information on her computer. "Oh," she says, "I'm sorry. We have to compound that. It won't be ready for pick up till tomorrow."

I blink. Then I start to cry. I feel like a complete idiot, standing there in the pharmacy, with tears streaming down my face. I can't even talk, because I know I'll sound hysterical, because I am hysterical.

The pharmacist puts her hand on my arm. "I'm so sorry," she says. "We'll have it ready first thing in the morning."

But it's not that, not really. It's that my nerves are shot from lack of sleep, from the stress of breastfeeding and pumping and bottle-feeding and trying to attend to Jack and Jane, too. It's that I don't have energy to pack all my kids into the sofa-mobile and drive them here tomorrow, and get them out of the car and schlep two car seats into the building and sit and wait another 45 minutes to pick up my prescription. It's that I desperately wanted this stuff today, wanted my nipples to stop aching all the flipping time, wanted some relief from just one damn thing in my life that is overwhelming me. It's that I completely wasted this last hour of my life when I could have been at home taking a nap.

The pharmacist is still patting my arm and looking at me, and I am still crying. I manage a weak smile through my tears and nod and whisper, "Thank you."

On the way home, I force myself to name ten graces in this situation. *James Herriot's book. Time with just Jane to read it. Luke didn't wake up the whole time we were at the pharmacy. It's sunny today. Julianne is watching Ben and Jack. My nipple cream will be ready in the morning.*

Doug will be home tonight. Dinner is already in the fridge, waiting only to be heated up. People from church—people I don't even know—are still bringing me meals every week.

By the time I get to number ten, I've managed to stop weeping. *That's eleven,* I tell myself. And by the time I get home, I've convinced myself that whether I freak out and get mad about this or not, I'm still going to have to go back to the pharmacy tomorrow, so I might as well do it cheerfully. I paste a smile I don't feel on my face and carry Luke into the house.

"I'm sorry that took so long," I tell Julianne.

She smiles at me. "Don't be. I'm just glad you were able to pick up your prescription."

I don't have the heart to tell her I didn't. So I just smile and nod and say, "Thank you."

"We had a lovely time." She hands Ben to me. "I gave him the bottle, but I think he's still hungry."

I force my smile to stay on my face, but inwardly I moan. Oh how I wish I'd been able to get that cream today. I look down at Ben, who is rooting around on my arm, and I sigh. There's nothing for it. The only way out is through. I get my nursing pillow and sit down with Ben on the sofa. *Tomorrow,* I tell myself. *Tomorrow and it will start to get better.* Ben latches on, and I wince and blink back tears. *I hope. Please, God.*

Ordinary Time
jackals
(october/november)

My soul clings to you;
    your right hand holds me fast.
May those who seek my life to destroy it
    go down into the depths of the earth;
let them fall upon the edge of the sword;
    and let them be food for jackals.

—Psalm 63

reflection

"This one's for you," Doug says as he comes into the kitchen with the mail.

I wipe my hands on my apron, which I have on over the Moby in which Luke is sleeping, and take the large envelope from him. "My articles!" I pull out three copies of the most recent issue of *Christian Reflection*.

Luke whimpers and I bounce a bit, since I can't pat his bum: my hands are full of journals, journals for which I wrote the introduction and a book review. I keep bouncing Luke as I stir the sausage around the pan with one hand and hold a journal in the other, reading the words I wrote back in June when I still had functional brain cells.

"I think they changed a bunch of stuff," I tell Doug after I finish the introduction.

"How so?"

I shrug. "I don't know. I don't really remember what I wrote, but they made me sound really good. Really smart."

"You are really smart."

"Not this smart." I hand him the journal and turn my attention back to dinner.

Later, after the babies are asleep and Jack and Jane are in bed, I flop onto the sofa with my computer to look at the drafts of the two articles I sent to the editor of *Christian Reflection* back in June and compare them with the printed version. My eyes go wide as I read. "They're the same," I say out loud. I look at Doug, sitting next to me. "They're the same. The editors didn't change anything." I grin big. "I really am that smart. I really am a good writer."

It doesn't feel like boasting. It feels like wonder. Those amazing words were words I had written. I feel blown away.

And giddy.

I remember how, a year ago, I was feeling so discouraged after my 19th agent rejection and another slew of magazine rejections, and then out of the blue, I got the email from *Christian Reflection*, asking me to write these two articles for their Advent issue this year. I remember how that night I'd stood in the bathroom watching myself in the mirror as I brushed my teeth, and I heard a voice in my head—my voice and yet not my voice—saying, *This is the way. Walk in it.* And I had. And now I am holding evidence of that journey in my hand in the form of these two articles, well-written and intelligent enough to amaze even their author.

"Oh Doug," I say and bury my face in his chest. "I can write. I can! I'm even good at it sometimes."

"You're good at it a lot of times," he says, "and you're getting better all the time."

"I want to write more," I say. "I want to do this again."

"You will." He smiles at me. "You will."

Tonight, I believe him. I believe that just as God provided this opportunity out of seemingly thin air, God will provide other opportunities. I trust Him. I trust His timing. I trust that He has given me this gift of words and will not fail to provide ways and places for me to use it for His glory and the good of His people.

At least, I trust tonight.

Tomorrow may be a different story.

grace notes, october 2

Making Doug laugh: when I lay nursing Luke (again!) this morning, he asked me how I felt. I said, "Like a mother pig." I think there might have been a trace of bitterness in my voice.

My morning cup of tea.

Sunshine. A walk with the kids every day for the past three days.

Reading to my children: we finished *On the Banks of Plum Creek*, and now we're reading *Little Pilgrim's Progress*.

A tea party on the lawn with Jane.

Apples fresh from the tree—so delicious.

Homemade bread with grape jelly that the kids and I made. (I'm still amazed by that.)

Bouquets of autumn crocuses, gifts from my children.

Luke's chronic look of delighted surprise—except when he's crying so hard his uvula quivers.

Ben's male pattern baldness. I'm not making this up: he has the hairline of a 70-year-old, and the hair he has is of the comb-over variety.

Jane hugs.

Jack kisses.

I got asked—asked!—to lead a breakout session at next year's Northwest Christian Writer's Conference.

Meals made for us every night this week. (What oh what am I going to do when it's my turn to start making our family's dinner each night?)

Jane's sleepy voice piping in the dark when I come to tuck her in: "Will you be right here and cuddle with me for a little second?"

A full moon rising in the east. Jupiter and Venus glowing like gems in the sky.

A clean kitchen at the end of the day. Admittedly, this doesn't happen every day, but I'm sure grateful when it does.

Daybreak. Even when it's a gray one.

the eve of seven

As I write these words, it is the last night Jack will be six. Come morning, he'll be a seven-year-old. Seven. No longer my baby, he's turning into a boy. I love the boy he's becoming, but I miss the baby and the child he was.

I miss cuddling in bed with him in my lap, reading stories for half the day.

I miss long, slow mornings at the zoo, hours spent watching the peacocks, waiting for them to open their tail feathers.

I miss yogurt and applesauce on the front porch after his nap.

I miss the words he used to mispronounce and the way he'd say "Bam" whenever he didn't know the answer to a question…or knew and wasn't telling.

I miss his lawn mower run, the way he'd jerk his right arm up and down like he was trying to start an old gas mower.

I miss chasing the recycling truck with him on spring afternoons, following behind it as it belched its way down the street.

I miss his little boy voice, the cadences and lilt of it that I can barely remember now.

I miss the softness of his hand in mine when we crossed the street.

Even though he's been healthy as a horse since we brought him home from the hospital seven years ago, I worry sometimes about him getting sick or, God forbid, dying. But what I'm beginning to see is that each day is a little death. Each day he grows a little older, a little further away from me. And that is natural and good. It is as it should be.

But I somehow didn't expect it. They forget to tell you when you're pregnant that motherhood is a long, slow process of letting go, a daily dying to what was in order to embrace what is. They forget to tell you how your heart breaks and breaks and keeps on breaking.

They forget to tell you how much it hurts to love a child.

But painful as the letting go is, I wouldn't trade my years with Jack for anything on this green earth or for all the stars in the sky. I can't say I've loved every minute of being his mom—there are quite I few I'd like to do over, for both our sakes—but I do love him. I love who he has been, I love who he's becoming.

So even though, on this last day of his seventh year, I weep because I miss him, because he's growing up; even though my heart aches and tears stream from my eyes, I wouldn't have it any other way. This ache, these tears say to me that my heart is still soft, and love grows in soft, broken places.

And how else should I live, except by loving? How could I not want a heart capable of deeper, richer love? A heart that holds Jack close and also lets him go? A heart that breaks with joy as well as pain? It is my prayer for his life, too: that all his days my beloved boy will know the joy and the ache of loving.

eat sleep bathe

The woman who ran our Expecting Multiples class emails me and asks if Doug and I would be willing to come talk to her next group of students. Poor suckers, they have the hellacious remainder of a twin pregnancy still ahead of them—not to mention those insane first weeks when your whole world turns on its axis about six times. For all I know, it starts revolving in reverse. That would explain a few things.

I read the email to Doug. "I'm not sure I'm the right person to talk to them," I tell him. "I'm a little bitter right now."

"No, you're a little tired right now. I think we're the perfect people to talk to them. We're right in the thick of it, and we can tell it like it is."

"We'll scare them."

"They should be scared. They should be very, very scared."

I make a face at him. Still, if we're going to do this, I want to tell them there are a few things they won't be able to do much of once their babies are born, things that are sort of important, things like eating and sleeping and bathing.

***

I've been feeling a bit dizzy and lightheaded the past few days. Being me, I of course immediately come to the only logical conclusion: I have a brain tumor.

When my mother-in-law shows up on Monday, she says I look a little peaked, and I tell her how dizzy I've been. She gently suggests that maybe I'm not drinking enough water. Might I be a little undernourished? Perhaps a little anemic?

I think about this. I am feeding three people after all, and I haven't been nearly as diligent about eating well postpartum as I was during my pregnancy. I haven't been drinking even close to the gallon of water a day that I'm supposed to. I haven't had more than a couple ounces of beef in the whole last week. And on Saturday when my symptoms started, I had biscuits with Nutella for lunch. Hm. Maybe she's on to something.

But I should still go in for a brain scan, just in case.

***

Also in the past few days, the boys have begun sleeping five hours at a stretch. This is more uninterrupted sleep than I've gotten since June when I couldn't sleep for the itching.

So I'm not sure why I'm so tired all of a sudden. Shouldn't I feel less tired since I'm getting more sleep?

Maybe it's the weather. And the shortening days.

Or maybe, as Doug's mom suggests, five months of poor sleep are bound to catch up with you sooner or later.

Or maybe I really do have a brain tumor.

***

I wake in the middle of the night. After registering the sound of a wailing infant, my next sensory awareness is of being cold. And clammy. This is one of the things I hate most about postpartum hormones: they make you sweat at night. In addition to the cold clamminess, I feel a puddle of sweat between my breasts, sitting like a little lake there on my breastbone. Totally gross.

But the worst of it is the smell. I reek. When did I shower last? I can't remember. Clearly, the brain tumor is affecting my memory.

The thing about sleeping is that you put your kids to bed every single night, and eventually you're so exhausted that you fall into bed at the same time. This keeps you at least somewhat rested—"rested" being a relative term, of course.

And the thing about eating is that every couple of hours your kids tell you that they're hungry and you have to make them food, so you may as well eat a handful of crackers with cheese or a peanut butter sandwich yourself. This keeps you from completely starving.

But those same kids aren't going to tell you to shower. In fact, they'd rather you didn't, since it often cuts in on their time with you, which is already pretty limited because of the babies. So sometimes, days will pass, and you will not get a chance to shower or you will take a nap instead of a shower or you will eat instead of showering. Then you will wake up in the middle of the night with a puddle of sweat between your breasts and a stench in your nostrils that horrifies even you.

I crawl out of bed, pick up the wailing baby, and start feeding him. Doug rolls out of the other side of the bed, gets a bottle and the other baby, and starts to feed him. After a few moments he says, "Um, would you mind taking a shower when you're done?"

"I was going to," I say, feeling stung, even though I wasn't.

But I do. At three in the morning, when I should be sleeping—everyone else in the house is asleep—I am awake, taking my first shower in only God knows how long.

***

"Okay," I say to Doug, "if we're going to go talk to these poor unsuspecting souls, we need to tell them to enjoy themselves now because once their babies are born, they can just forget about eating and sleeping and bathing."

"And having sex," Doug says.

"Sex?" I say. "What's that?"

"Exactly." He pulls me into his lap. "Maybe you could remind me."

"No chance, pal. That's what got us into this mess in the first place."

okay

Margie and I sit silently in the little room off her back porch where we always meet for spiritual direction. Her eyes are closed. Mine are open. I stare out the window at the gray sky. The cup of tea I hold warms my hands, but anxiety clutches my chest in its icy grip.

"In the name of the Father, the Son, and the Holy Spirit," Margie says quietly and opens her eyes. She watches me a moment—I can feel her gaze—and then says what she always says, "Where has God been meeting you this past month?"

I tell her about the articles in *Christian Reflection*, about my delighted surprise that they were so good. "I didn't know I had that many working neurons back in June. It's not even six months ago, Margie, and I feel like my entire brain has atrophied."

She smiles. I'm exaggerating, and she knows it.

"I want to write," I say. "Another novel. I've never felt as alive as I did when I was working on my novel. But who has time? I know the day is coming—" I turn my eyes to the ceiling and the sky beyond "—soon, please, God—" I look back at Margie "—when the twins will sleep through the night. When I will, too. When I won't be so flipping tired all the time." I take a sip of tea. "I'm trying to be patient, trying to stay here in the present. So I keep blogging—it's the only writing outlet I have energy for right now." I shrug. "But I'm struggling to find my voice. I'm struggling to know why I write and what I should be writing and what the point of it is. I'm struggling to even know what 'my writing' is—because it's all over the map. And I'm tired of being so diffuse."

I roll my eyes. "So what did I go and do? I had two more kids. Yeah, *that'll* help me focus."

I take a breath and say softly, "It's hard sometimes not to wish things were different, not to wish I still only had two children." I look up at Margie. "I love Luke and Ben. I do."

She nods. "Of course you do."

"Especially now that they're smiling and making all those fun baby noises and not just wailing all the time." I smile weakly. "But it's still a lot of work." I exhale loudly. "And it will continue to be a lot of work, and it's hard for me to accept that this is my life right now—being tired to the point of tears. Feeling fuzzy-brained." I take another sip of tea. "Feeling anxious all the time."

Margie nods. She understands anxiety. It's her demon, too.

"I think that's the worst part," I say. "I hate the way it chokes me and pushes tears to my eyes. I hate the tightness that's always sitting right here like a rock or a vise." I place a hand over my chest and take a deep breath, trying to force the anxiety away with oxygen. "I hate feeling afraid all the time. I want to live expansively, you know? With my hands and heart open. I want to not be so afraid."

I look out the window again and take a sip of my tea. It's still hot and sears my throat a little as I swallow it. I wish it would sear the anxiety right out of my chest. "My life is so good." I look back at Margie, and I feel like I'm pleading with her to understand, even though I don't understand myself. "So good. So many gifts. So much to be grateful for and rejoice in and celebrate. So why am I so scared so much of the time? Why this constant battle against anxiety?"

Margie's eyes are kind. "Oh, Kimberlee, I wish I knew. I wish I understood why some of us struggle so much with fear, why..." her voice trails off. "Why don't we sit for a moment in silence? See if God might speak to us or show himself to us in the midst of your anxiety and your longing to write?"

I nod. Silence is always good, and I get so little of it at home. I set my tea on the table beside me and close my eyes, my hands resting, palms up, in my lap.

Lord, your love is perfect. Your love is perfect. It casts out fear. Cast out my fear. Heal me of this anxiety. I get so scared of all that can go wrong. Help me to see all that is right and good and beautiful. Help me to search

*out such things. Cast out my fear and in its place, plant joy. Please. God.
Please.*

The *please, God, please* echoes in my thoughts that swirl around and
around, like clothes in the washing machine or the dryer, whirling,
whirling, which makes me think of the washed but still unfolded laundry that defeats me before a new day has even dawned gray and overcast—looming on the dining room table like a hulking monster, where
I'd moved it the night before so I could actually sleep in my bed—and
I wonder if I'm ever going to get on top of that pile and vanquish it, or
if it will be sitting there on the table by night and on my bed by day,
mocking me till the day I die.

And the anxiety grips harder—*please, God, please*—as I recall my diz-
ziness and light-headedness of the past few days, the way I keep forget-
ting things, or breaking off in the middle of a sentence because I can't
for the life of me remember what I was going to say and it makes me so
scared I have a brain tumor or the beginning of some horrible degenera-
tive disease. *Please, God, please, cast out my fear.*

In my mind's eye I see a montage of the babies, wailing, wailing,
wailing, and me, inept and impotent, unable to comfort them, unable
to comfort myself, and Jack and Jane looking worried when I can't keep
the tears back any longer and start to cry, too, weeping right along with
the boys. And I see my breast pump bottles, with only three ounces of
milk in them each time I pumped the past three days, and I feel the
anxiety tighten its vise as I worry that my milk supply is failing and I
hear Doug's rational reassurance and I know he's right, that it's okay,
that even if it's not okay, there's always formula, but it doesn't help—the
anxiety squeezes so hard it gnaws at my gut and no amount of rational
discourse on the part of my reasonable and patient husband can make it
go away. And then Doug goes away. Every morning he leaves for work
and it's gray or raining outside and the whole day stretches before me
and I don't know how I'm going to make it through, and I flail and
tears press hard in my throat, in my eyes, and Jack and Jane watch me,
worried. *Please, God, please.*

"Margie?" I say.

She opens her eyes.

"I don't think this is helping. I can't get hold of my thoughts. They're
churning, and I just feel more anxious the more I sit here and churn."

She nods. "So what would be helpful, do you think?"

I shake my head. "I don't know." I spill the crazy spiral of my thoughts into her ear.

She listens. When I'm through, she leans forward. "But Kimberlee, even in the midst of all this, you're doing the things you need to do, don't you see? You're breastfeeding the babies. You're caring for Jack and Jane. You're even praying—all those *please God*'s—that's prayer."

I blink at her.

"I know that doesn't help with the anxiety much, but it shows me how strong you are. How faithful."

The anxiety relaxes just a little. "I'm still taking grace notes," I say. "I'm still writing them down."

She smiles. "That's prayer, too, Kimberlee."

"It helps," I say. "A little. With the anxiety. I mean, it doesn't really make it go away, but it keeps me grounded in the present, in what's happening now, so I don't flee ahead so much. And right now, right here? I'm okay." I shrug. "Well, mostly. Sometimes."

Margie smiles.

And even though the anxiety still grips hard, I manage to smile back at her.

food for jackals

"We come now to a time of silent confession," our associate pastor, Renee, says from the lectern at the front of the church. "Let's pray."

I sit in the pew, anxiety gnawing at my stomach and sitting stone-like on my chest, and for the first time in my life, I confess my anxiety. I've never seen it as sin before; it's just a part of me. I remember the words I typed in an article for the church newsletter years ago, words of Victor-Antoine D'Avila-Latourrette, about sins that have become so encrusted in our personalities that we no longer recognize them for what they are. That's just it. Anxiety is so encrusted in my personality that I don't even see it as sin. It's just part of who I am. But if sin is simply something that separates me from God, my anxiety definitely qualifies. It keeps me from seeing God. It undermines my fragile trust in Him.

Seeing it this way changes everything: anxiety is no longer simply a personality thing; it becomes a relationship thing, a bad relationship thing because it hinders my relationship with Christ. The desert fathers were right to classify fear as the root of all the eight demons. And my anxiety is simply a physiological manifestation of fear. So I confess it. I ask Jesus to forgive me for giving in to it so often. I ask Him to help me overcome this demon, so I can live in freedom rather than fear.

So easy to say, so hard to do.

I am grateful for years of freedom from the chronic anxiety that I used to carry around with me like some kind of ball and chain. But all these months of sleep-deprivation are catching up with me, and I am fighting anxiety harder these past few months than I have for years.

And I hate it. I hate that feeling of heaviness in my chest, the sense that I'm struggling to draw breath, and the tears that force themselves to the surface when I feel this way. I hate the way it robs me of life, of joy, of delight because I'm spending so much energy just trying to keep it from overwhelming me. I hate it.

So I sit in the pew and I confess it. And I recite the last verses of Psalm 63. Again.

***

Two weeks ago, as I fought to free myself of this weight, I read Psalm 63 during morning prayer, and these words leaped out at me:

My soul clings to you;
your right hand holds me fast.
May those who seek my life to destroy it
go down into the depths of the earth;
let them fall upon the edge of the sword
and let them be food for jackals.
But I will rejoice in God.

Ordinarily, such invectives make me highly uncomfortable; I like to think I'm a peaceable person, opposed to violence and vengeance. I'm fully aware that I'm both delusional and a hypocrite: I regularly indulge in revenge fantasies about the agents who rejected my novel, as well as vindictive thoughts about writers who, in my humble opinion, don't deserve the success they've achieved. Nothing so violent as feeding them to jackals, of course, but a little verbal swordplay in which I emerge the victor is always soothing to the ego.

But suddenly, these words were not about agents or writers or even about people. For me, just then, the enemy was Anxiety.

Anxiety seeks my life to destroy it.

I wept. Then I prayed these words, hard. I wrote them on a note card and taped it to my kitchen window. I read and re-read them. I memorized them. I kept praying them—my way, I suppose, of clinging to God, whose right hand holds me fast.

***

Sitting in church, my head bowed so that my hair hides the tears that are streaming down my face, I pray those words again. Then I start to number the graces the day has brought—tea and toast with Doug, my church community who is still bringing me meals and who holds me in the exhausted blur that my life has become, this moment of silence, the relief and release that tears bring—and the anxiety lifts from my chest a little, and I take a deep breath.

And later, twice—once on our walk to the park when I spy a bare birch tree in brilliant white relief against the blue, blue sky and then, again, at the park when I hear Jane shriek with delight as Doug pushes her high high high in the swing—I feel, in the place where the anxiety usually sits, something that I can only call joy bubble up.

I can't help but laugh. Doug turns to look at me, and we smile at each other. Then I tear off across the park in pursuit of Jack, who runs shrieking gleefully away from me.

It feels good to feed the jackals.

spoonful

It's a sunny day, and warm. Tiffany and I are down at the lake—we walked here from her house, all seven of our kids in tow. The older four—even Michaela, with her skinny white legs sticking out from under her rolled-up leggings and a warm cap pulled over her bald head—wade in the water.

Tiffany and I sit on a blanket a ways away, near enough to see the kids, far enough to chat openly without being overheard. The twins sleep in the stroller. Tiffany leans against a tree and nurses Emily.

"How are you?" she asks me. "I mean, how are you really?"

I shrug. "Anxious."

"Me, too."

I reach over and give her forearm a little squeeze. "Oh friend, I know you are. I think some of my anxiety is for you."

We both look over to the shore. Michaela kicks a shower of water with her foot. She and Jane squeal.

"She looks really good," I say.

"She's so skinny," Tiffany says. "She's still not eating."

In addition to the port in her chest where she gets all her medication, Michaela also has a tube through her nose into her stomach. She gets almost all her nutrition that way. I can't imagine how hard this is for Tiffany, to watch this disease emaciate her daughter.

"It shakes your faith, you know?" Tiffany says. "To see children suffer." She shakes her head. "The thing is, children are always suffering, all over the world, they're dying of hunger or malaria or whatever. And that

bothered me, of course, but it never made me question God's goodness.
It never shook my faith like this does."

I nod. I know. Michaela's leukemia has thrown me for a faith loop,
too.

"If we lived somewhere else," Tiffany continues, "instead of here in
the States, Michaela would be dying, just like all those other kids who
don't have access to clean water or enough food or decent doctors. It's
only because we have access to some of the best health care in the world
that she's not."

I sit mutely, watching Tiffany watch Michaela.

Tiffany gives me a weak smile. "Don't get me wrong. I'm so grateful
that we're the lucky ones, that Michaela's prognosis is so good, that
it's not 20 years ago, and that we live here, now. There's so much to be
thankful for."

I nod. "But it's still hard."

"Yes," Tiffany says, "it's still hard."

I watch Jack and Madeline, crouching at the water's edge. They
brought string with them from the house, and they're using it to tie
rocks and leaves and twigs together.

I think of my own fears of late, all the anxiety swirling around inside
me for no good reason. I think of how it has me making up reasons
to explain it—I'm sick, I'm dying, my breast milk is failing, my career
is failing, I'm psychic and am having a premonition of bad things to
come. I think how paying attention to God's graces in the midst of the
fear helps…but it doesn't change the situation itself. Michaela still has
leukemia. I still battle anxiety. My book is still tanking. My novel still
lies untouched in the basement.

I think of my mom in the long months of my dad's unemployment
last year, how she was always looking ahead eagerly, anticipating the
ways God was going to provide for their financial needs—a few days of
contract work, a gift from their church—and always, like the widow of
Zarepheth, they had enough.

I want to be like Mama, eager, anticipating God's provision, trusting
Him to provide all that we need—and even more. I know this does
not mean that He will give me what I want or even what I ask for, but
it does mean He will provide for me, for our family. I think back to
when Ben was at Children's and those scary few days when we didn't

know if he was even going to make it, and in those days, even though I was afraid he might die, I wasn't afraid God wasn't good. I knew in my bones that if God chose not to heal Ben, we would still trust Him; we would still believe in His goodness.

So why do I fear and doubt now? I'm not sure, but I am convinced that such anxiety is a tool of the evil one, and I pray those words from Psalm 63, that God would deliver me from the anxiety that seeks my life to destroy it. I want to be free of this. I want God's victory in my life over the fear—this sin that so easily entangles me, tying me in knots and preventing me from reaching out in love and trust that all shall be well. I don't want to live like this. I want to laugh again and to revel in the goodness of life. And even to rejoice in the midst of difficulty, to remember that Jesus is with me and will never forsake me and His perfect love casts out my fear. I don't know how to live such a life, how to rejoice when I am sad or scared. But I want to learn. I want to live.

"Mama, look!" Jack and Madeline walk toward where Tiffany and I sit on the blanket. They're each carrying something cradled in the palm of one hand.

"Look, Mom!" Madeline holds out…a spoon. Jack, too.

"You made this?" Tiffany asks.

Both kids grin and nod. Down at the beach, they tied a stick and a leaf together and made a perfect spoon.

I look at it in wonder. A spoon. It is the perfect image for my life. I cannot handle the vastness of life. My borrowing imaginary trouble from the future is like gulping the whole of Lake Washington. I cannot do it. I can only take a spoonful at a time, a sip, this moment, and now this one, and now this one. God gives me strength to manage the spoonful of today's troubles. One spoonful at a time, I can drink the cup of my life.

Jack places his spoon in my hand, and the sun strikes the green of the leaf.

"It's beautiful, Jack." And it is. Still more graces to note: a leaf spoon shining in the sun, and the boy who made it, and the God who spoke to me through it.

four

Jane turns four tomorrow. I confess, I'm a little surprised that she's just now four: she's so tall, so articulate, so mature, I often forget she's only three. I hope she'll forgive me for the times this year when I forgot how young she was and so expected more from her than she could give.

I'm sure I'll forget again, because she's still tall and articulate and mature. But we've both grown up some this past year, so maybe I won't forget so often. Or maybe she'll rise to the occasion. Or maybe we'll just muddle through and make the best of things: grace abounds in our relationship, in both directions, because her heart is large and my heart is for her.

As this new year of her life begins, these are some of the things I want to remember about my dear sweet girl, about the three-year-old she was:

All last fall, and through the winter until my belly grew too big, she fell asleep in my bed each night, lying on my chest. When I'd pick her up to take her to her bed, she'd wrap her little legs around my waist, her arms around my neck, and sometimes she'd sigh in her sleep, whisper "I love you, Mama," against my shoulder, and I'd think every time I carried her that the weight of her in my arms was perfect.

She loves to run. I love to watch her, the way her little feet pound the ground, her strong legs pumping, her golden hair streaming out behind her.

She always mispronounces the word "pajamas." She says "tajamas" instead. And callapitter. And cimmanin. I'm dreading the day she outgrows this.

One night last month, when I came to tuck her in after I'd fed the babies at three a.m., she woke up just enough to say, "Will you cuddle with me right here for a little minute?" Though I was bone tired, how could I say no? I lay down beside her, and she put her hand in mine, and we both fell asleep.

On our daily walks through the neighborhood, Jane is always calling, "Look, Mama!" and pointing out tulips in bloom or roses or dahlias or little johnny-jump-ups growing next to the sidewalk or the scarlet or yellow or sienna leaves of an autumn tree. "Isn't it pretty?" she says.

And I say, "Yes," but I don't say how grateful I am that she notices these things, that she's teaching me to notice them, too.

Once, not long ago, when I gave Jane her bedtime blessing in the name of the Trinity, she told me soberly, thoughtfully, "God is our Father in Heaven, and Jesus is God on earth, and the Spirit is God in our hearts." And I wondered how she knows this, who taught her, and how she came to be a theologian at the age of three.

When she bought her first 200-piece puzzle, she cried because it was too hard for her—the first time, I think, that she couldn't do a puzzle by herself. Doug and I sat down and helped her with it that first time. After that, she hasn't needed us to help her anymore. But sometimes she wants us to.

Though I can't hold on to the feeling of her hand in mine, I want always to remember that her hands are soft and warm and trusting when she slips them into my mine.

Though I won't remember the sweet sound of her little voice, I want to remember that every day for the past nine months she has faithfully prayed for Michaela. Four times a day—once at each meal and again at bedtime—she prays a prayer of thanksgiving for Michaela and for God's healing of her. Oh, that I had her faith!

And I want to remember holding her while she cried because she'd fallen out of bed, or knocked her tooth against the arm of the sofa, or left her brand-new toy that she bought with her own money in the grocery store. I want to remember that she trusted me and that sometimes, I deserved her trust and responded to her pain the right way— with hugs and kisses and love and my own tears.

On this last night that she is three, she falls asleep in my bed. When I pick her up to carry her from my bed to hers, I notice that she's grown—a lot. Her legs around my waist are longer; her body, heavier. But she puts her arms around my neck and breathes softly against my cheek, and the weight of her is still perfect.

grace notes, november 5

It's rained all weekend. A lot. I've sat on the sofa for much of today, either nursing the babies or reading to my older kids or (amazingly!) reading to myself. I've even gotten to journal.

My anxiety level has been a little lower today, maybe a four on a scale of ten. I don't know why. I don't really care. I'll take it, and gladly.

The rain drips off the leaves of the spirea bush outside the living room window, the water drops hanging like little pearl beads on the thin branches, the red and yellow leaves vibrant against the gray day.

Somewhere outside, a crow caws.

Jack and Jane sit at the dining room table, bickering about who gets to be what color in Sorry. Jack chooses blue, Jane chooses red, and they give me green.

Doug stands over the stove, making quesadillas. The babies sleep. The heat rattles in the registers, warming the house. Outside, the day is quiet except for the soft steady hush of the rain.

I sit on the sofa and look at it all, listen to it all, notice it all: the gift that is my life. It's a quiet life—well, except when one or more of my children is crying, and even then, it's a good life.

And I am grateful.

remember this night

On a rainy Sunday in November, Renee stands in front of the communion table and holds up the chalice and the plate of bread. "Remember this night," she says. "Remember this night whenever you think something is impossible."

My life is impossible. I feel anxious. A gaping ache in my chest. And I don't know why. I cannot live like this. I have to live like this. Because this is my life right now: sleeplessness, exhaustion, anxiety.

"Remember this night," Renee says again. "The night of the Passover. The night of Good Friday. The night of Holy Saturday." She holds the elements aloft, and I weep, thinking of God watching His beloved Son suffer and die. I weep, thinking of all the hurting children and their hurting parents. Tiffany and Michaela. A girl they know from Children's, who is five and has an inoperable brain tumor and six months to live. Little Finn, four months old, at Children's at the same time as Ben, whose mother hadn't held him in weeks. And every mother of every child who, like Mary, has to hold her dead child in her arms. I weep for them all, and for my own fear of such suffering coming to me.

"Remember this night," Renee says, "the night of Easter, when the disciples on the road to Emmaus recognized our risen Lord in the breaking of the bread."

I feel like broken bread, like a loaf split right down the center, crumbs scattered. *Gather up the fragments.* The words come to my mind like a soft quilt, wrapping me in a moment of warmth. Nothing will be lost. I weep. I want so desperately for that to be true, for Jesus to gather up the scattered crumbs of my thoughts, my emotions, my life and make me whole again, restore me to myself.

"Because of the broken body of Christ raised and restored," Renee says, "nothing is impossible with God. Nothing." She looks right at me. "Nothing." She smiles warmly at the congregation. "Christ leads us through grief to glory. And He invites all who would draw near to Him to come to this table and taste and see that the Lord is good."

The Lord is good. I believe this. I do. Oh, Jesus, help my unbelief. Help me to believe that when suffering comes to me, as it must, that you will strengthen me to bear it. I stand and move to the center aisle, begin to make my way to the front of the church to receive the body and blood. *Help me to believe that simply bearing my current fatigue and anxiety with grace, bearing the busyness of life with twin babies, bearing the loneliness and the insignificance, and the tiredness and the daily letting go of my husband and my children and my writing and the life I thought I'd have— help me to believe that bearing this is enough for this season.*

Renee places a wafer in my upturned palm. "Kimberlee, the body of Christ was broken for you."

I dip the wafer into the cup.

"The blood of Christ was poured out for you."

I put the juice-soaked wafer into my mouth. It's so little. It's so not enough. Into my mind comes the memory of those scary days when Ben was at Children's with the ECMO machine beside his bed, when we weren't sure he was going to live, and I remember that I wasn't anxious then, not like this. I was afraid, and my heart hurt, but I was also, in a way, relieved—relieved that when my fears were realized, when suffering came, I was able to bear it. I saw the very real possibility that I could be a woman whose child has died—and I was okay. I still cried out to God to remove that cup. And He did. But even if He hadn't, even if Ben had died, I knew that we would still believe that God is good. *Oh Jesus, restore that faith to me! I am so afraid. I am afraid to suffer.*

The wafer dissolves on my tongue. I swallow it down.

writing

I can't stop crying. So I pick up my journal and begin to write.

Ben, the blessed boy, slept eight hours last night. I think he's my favorite twin. Luke slept six. So: I got six hours of uninterrupted sleep last night. You'd think I'd feel great. I don't. I feel as tired as ever. And weepy as all get out. I need a month of this kind of sleep to feel rested. Maybe more.

Laura picked Jack and Jane up this morning to take them swimming at the Y with Ryan and Ella, to give me a few minutes to myself, she said. Her marriage is imploding, and *she's* taking care of *me*. The babies are quietly lying on the floor, deathgripping their plush toys and drooling on them. It's a gift to have a few moments of silence.

But—I fall apart in the silence. It gives me space to feel, and I don't want to feel, because mostly when I'm away from the kids, what I feel is fear. What if something happens to them? A car accident? A drowning accident? What if they die and I never see them again?

I am so afraid. It overwhelms me, the fear.

I have to stop fleeing ahead. I have to stay here, now.

Writing out the fear helps. Tremendously. It helps me stop crying. It helps me stop feeling overwhelmed. It provides focus for my swirling thoughts and disciplines them, forcing them into a single channel where I can attend to them. When I'm not writing and I'm just thinking and feeling diffusely, that's when I get overwhelmed. That's when I get anxious and afraid. That's when my not being capable, my not being enough gets to me and makes me cry and fear and rage. That's when my fear of suffering and death and my dreams never coming true rushes through me like a tornado, strewing anxiety and chills and weak limbs in its wake. I still feel sick to my stomach as I write, but I'm not crying. I'm not overwhelmed. The act of putting pen to paper and stringing words in ink along the page focuses my thoughts, forces them to march in a line instead of whirling around like the straight between Scylla and Charybdis.

I am okay when I write. The anxiety lessens some. The landmines in my mind are not buried in this channel in which I write. They're off to the side somewhere, in the No Man's Land that my brain has become after six months of crazy hormonal fluxes and insane-making sleep-deprivation. Writing keeps my thoughts from setting off the mines.

The problem is: I can't keep writing forever. Luke is starting to fuss and needs a nap before he falls apart. There are dishes to be done and clothes to fold—piles and piles of them. And when I leave the page, my thoughts spin out of control, bouncing out of this controlled channel, setting off explosions of panic that shatter through my body like so much shrapnel and I start to be afraid again that I am going to die, that the kids are going to die, and that the whole Christian promise is a joke or a lie or the deluded fantasy of weak and needy people who simply want to believe that we will see our lost loved ones again, that death is not the end. That fear is not the end.

That's what this all boils down to: I'm afraid God is not. And writing is the only way I know to channel my thoughts so that I remember what I believe, so that I cling to the hope that God is.

Perhaps this is why Paul exhorts us to pray without ceasing: because prayer—the mindful attention to one stream of thought, directed God-ward—is like writing; it channels our wayward thoughts, our diffuse emotions, so they do not overwhelm us. Plus, prayer places us at the feet of Jesus who intercedes for us with the Father, asking for all we need, transforming our prayers into Prayer.

Oh Jesus, take my heart, my mind, my thoughts, my feelings and rein them in. Reign in them. Reign over them. Channel them into manageability. And give me strength to meet the demands of this day. Keep me here in the present. Keep me from fleeing ahead. Give me your peace that passes all understanding. Guard my heart and my mind.

I don't want to stop writing. I don't want the thoughts to crowd back in.

But Luke is getting fussy, and he's going to start wailing if I don't stop moving my pen across the page and put him to bed. Deep breath. Just breathe. Breathe.

Lord Jesus Christ, Son of God, have mercy on me.

minus thirteen

I open the envelope from my publisher. Inside is my royalty statement for the year ending June 30th. I sold -13 books last year. *Minus 13.*

"Why did I even bother?" I wave the statement at Doug. "I poured my heart and soul into this book and for what? For minus 13! *Minus 13!* I spent a year of my life on that book. Wasted a year of my life, is more like it."

He looks at me. "You think so?" His voice is gentle. "You think it was wasted?"

I look down at the royalty statement and shake my head. "I wanted to write another book," I say sadly. "No one will ever publish me again. Not with abysmal numbers like this." I look at him. "Am I delusional? Maybe it really wasn't very good."

Doug says, "You don't believe that."

He's right. I don't. "But what's the point of writing well if no one reads it?"

"Do you think it's worth it?"

I shrug.

"Then why do you write?"

"I can't help it." The words come out half-whine, half-wail.

He knows this, of course. I'm the one who needs a reminder. Even if I never write another word on paper or a screen, I'll always be writing in my head. I don't live, really, unless I'm writing. Words are how I see things.

"I love writing," I say.

"I know you do." Doug wraps his arms around me. "The question isn't whether you love writing. It's do you want a writing career? You can write all you want, but if you're not willing to market what you write—" he shrugs "—then you're not going to have a writing career. You can't have the career without the marketing."

I lean against his shoulder. A year ago, I desperately wanted to be a multipublished author—an Author—someone who always has a contract in hand. Or I thought I did. But Doug's right: I don't want to have to market the books I write.

And until I'm willing to, I'd best get used to negative sales.

"This completely sucks," I say against Doug's sweater.

"Yes," he says, "it does. You've never been one to choose the easy path." He tips my head back so he can see my face. "It's one of the things I love most about you."

I manage a weak smile. "Well, that's something, anyway."

screaming

It's 5:45 p.m., and I've bathed Jane, who is, admittedly, still running around the house in her towel, but hey, at least she's clean. Jack is in the tub, scrubbing himself. Ben is in his crib, asleep. Luke is in the Moby, alternately wailing and whimpering on my chest. Dinner is bubbling on the stove.

I stir the pasta sauce with a wooden spoon and pat Luke's bum with my other hand. I think I might finally be getting the hang of this whole life-with-four-children thing.

I smile.

It slowly dawns on me that Jane isn't running around anymore. In fact, it's suddenly quiet, except for Luke's cries. Then, I hear giggles. Loud giggles. From the bathroom. Silence followed by laughter is always, always, a combination to be feared.

I head to the bathroom, my mad face already on. I don't know what they've done, but I know I'm not going to like it.

Jane stands by the tub, her towel still wrapped around her. She leans over, lets the towel fall into the water, then jumps back, flinging water everywhere. She and Jack erupt into laughter. Fully a quarter of her towel is wet—no, soaked—and it's making a small lake on the tile.

"What are you doing?" I bellow above Luke's crying.

They both look up, the delight on their faces vanishing.

"I'm sorry, Mama," Jane says, and tries to run from the room.

"NO!" I say and grab her before she can get to the door. "You'll just make a water mess out there! Clean it up!" I jab my finger at the floor.

She stares at me. "I said clean it up! Now!" I yell. "Get a towel and clean it up!"

Jane starts to cry. Luke wails in the Moby. Water puddles on the tile. My socks are wet.

I turn on my heel and march out of the bathroom. I hate wet socks. I stand in the dining room and scream. I scream so loud and so long that Luke stops screaming. He's that shocked.

I'm shocked, too. Did I really just do that? Really? Who's supposed to be the adult around here anyway?

It's just water. It's not hard to clean up. The floor is covered with sealed tile. Why oh why do I get so bent out of shape over stupid things like a puddle of water on the bathroom floor? Who cares? I mean, who other than me? And why do I care anyway? Jack and Jane are fully capable of cleaning up a water mess. It's really not my problem…or it wouldn't be, except that I freak out and throw a temper tantrum and make a bigger mess, a mess in my children's hearts, in their souls.

I peel off my wet socks and throw them in the laundry. Barefoot, I go back to the bathroom where both kids are trying to mop up the water on the floor. I sit on the toilet lid. I say, "I'm sorry." I don't have more words than that. I mean, what can you say when you're 35 and behave like a three-year-old?

Jack says, "It's my fault, Mama. I told her to do it. Don't be mad at Jane."

I shake my head. "I'm mad at me. I'm sorry I got so angry. I'm sorry I yelled at you guys. I'm sorry I screamed."

Jane gives me a hug. "It's okay, Mama. I love you."

Tears prick at my eyes. Why couldn't I be the one to say those words? To look at the puddle on the floor and say to my children, "It's okay. I love you"?

I wrap my children in my arms. They're still wet, and they soak the Moby, but it's okay. I love them. And someday, please God, someday, I will remember that in the very moment that I walk in on a mess, and in that moment, I will say, "It's okay. I love you."

Until then, I'm just going to have to keep saying, "I'm sorry."

fear not

On Sunday, Julianne preaches about faith and fear. She asks, "Where in our lives are we living in fear instead of faith?"

I ask, Where in my life am I not living in fear?

I am afraid we will never pay off the hospital bills and the car loan and we'll have to live in this tiny house for the rest of our lives or that if we do pay them off, by the time we manage to save enough to afford a larger house, we'll all be stark raving mad.

I am afraid I have brain cancer and that I'm going to die and my children won't even remember me and they'll wander through their lives with a mama-shaped hole in their hearts.

I am afraid Doug will die and I will have to raise four children on my own.

I am afraid that one of my kids will drown. Or get sick. Or injured. Or maimed. Or molested. Or kidnapped.

I am afraid my publisher is going to take my book out of print.

I am afraid I will never write another book. Or that if do write one, it won't get published. Or if it gets published, it won't sell and will get remaindered.

I am afraid that people look at me and think what a wreck I am and how glad they are that they're not me. Or that they look at me and think what a sniveling whiner I am and don't I see how good my life is and what is my problem anyway?

I am afraid that I will be this effing tired for the rest of my mortal life.

I guess you could say I spend, oh, about half of my time and energy being afraid. And time and energy are two things that are in really low supply in my life these days. So this kind of makes me mad, you know? That I'm wasting these two precious, scarce commodities being afraid.

I know all the right answers, about how I shouldn't borrow trouble, about how living in the present is the only place I'm okay and how I really am okay as long as I stay right here right now, about how God's grace is sufficient for this day but like manna won't last till morning or get me through whatever I fear tomorrow will bring, about how I'm totally wasting energy worrying and being afraid, about how it only robs me of joy in the present, etc., etc., ad infinitum.

I know all this stuff. But I've got 35 years of habitually anxious thought patterns to overcome if I'm going to live it, and for some inexplicable reason I'm a little tired these days and am not firing with both barrels at the anxiety demon that preys on my fear.

So when I get home from church, I write the Bible's number-one-most-repeated commandment and stick it on my kitchen window. It's not "Love God" or "Love others." It's "Fear not." When God and the angels show up, that's what they always say to people.

Fear not.

Fear is what the anxiety demon always tries to fan into flame.

I write "FEAR NOT" in all caps on two note cards and tape them to my kitchen window, to remind me that fear is not from God and I don't have to live with it or in it.

But that doesn't seem to be enough. So I write these words, in large caps, each on a separate note card, as a reminder and a promise to myself, and tape them underneath FEAR NOT:

I WILL NOT BE AFRAID.

I will not be afraid. Because I am so tired of being afraid. Because I am so tired of missing out on the joy of now when I fear the future. Because I am just plain tired and don't have energy to waste on fear.

It's starting to piss me off, actually. I have such a good life. Yeah, it has its moments. But they're just moments. On the whole, I probably have one of the best lives in human history. Health (well, except for the brain cancer), wealth (except for the small house), food to eat (if only I had time), a beautiful healthy family, friends who love me, a church community who cares for me. I mean, really. It doesn't get a whole lot better than this. And if it all disappeared tomorrow, I would have missed it because I was so afraid it would all disappear tomorrow.

So.

I will not be afraid.

I will not be afraid.

I. Will. Not. Be. Afraid.

That anxiety demon can go to hell.

***

Two weeks later, Susan comes over for dinner. She stands with me in the kitchen while I make salad. "How's it going?" She points at the note cards taped to the kitchen window frame.

I smile weakly. "It's one thing to write it down. It's another to live it." I breathe deep as I slice kale leaves off their stems. My fears about my health, my life, my future were in full force yesterday. Thanks be to God, they're quieter and more manageable today. My emotions change, quite literally, with the weather. I say, "I still feel fuzzy-headed and even dizzy sometimes."

Susan knows this scares me. She says, "You know that's only to be expected, right? You're not exercising. You're not sleeping enough. You're not eating enough."

She's right. I'm supposed to have ten cups of milk a day and three ounces of beef or pork. I'm barely getting half that, and I'm breastfeeding two rapidly growing babies, who are sucking the life out of me. I'm also not sleeping enough. And I'm not exercising at all. I haven't been for a walk since the weather turned cold and rainy, close to a month ago.

Susan says, "The lack of that trinity of basics affects executive function, Kimberlee. Severely."

I toss kale leaves into the salad bowl and shake my head. "Susan, my brain is so cracked I don't even know what executive function means anymore. Assuming I ever did."

She grins. "It just means the ability to focus and think clearly."

"Oh," I say. "So you're saying that if my executive function were working properly I wouldn't be so worried that I have cancer?"

She nods. "Basically."

Tears prick my eyes. I blink them away and force myself to focus on the kale. My back to Susan, I say softly, "My fear of cancer is really a fear of dying." I swallow against the tightness in my throat. "A fear of the unknown, but also a fear of being forgotten, especially by my children." I can no longer see the kale leaves for the tears swimming in my eyes. I hold the knife gingerly. "I feel like Jesus has been asking me: do you love me more than these? And I've had to say no. I want to love Jesus more. I don't want my children to become idols in my life. But they are. They are. I love them so much, and I can't imagine life without them." My voice cracks and I can barely whisper the last word.

Susan puts her hand on my arm. "I don't think you need to be worried about your children becoming idols. I think you might instead see them as revelations of God's love to you."

The tears spill over, coursing down my cheeks. I set down the knife and wipe them away.

Susan continues, "Besides, Eugene Peterson says that prayer is the answer to the idolatry in our lives. He says prayer returns God to his rightful place at the center. And Kimberlee, you pray. You pray all the time. Those verses from Psalm 63—" she gestures toward the note card taped to the kitchen window "—that's prayer. Even your desire to not have your children be idols is a kind of prayer—it shows that your heart is in the right place, that you want God to be at the center. And this pleases Him."

More tears fall. I wipe them away, too. I hope she's right.

"And even if you die, or your kids die, there's joy beyond the grief. That's what Jesus promises. That's what it means to believe in Him, that there's always joy on the other side of pain."

I want so desperately for that to be true, and I am so afraid it's not. I want to crumple up into a little ball right here on the kitchen floor and weep my fear away. I don't. I manage a wobbly smile at Susan and pick up the knife and finish prepping the kale.

grace notes, thanksgiving day

Snow last night.

Bread rising on the stove.

Ben's joyful, laughing smiles.

This moment of quiet: snow falling gently, the rattle of the heat registers, Jane's quiet voice as she "reads" *Prince Caspian*, a warm fuzzy blanket spread over my lap.

Right here, right now, for this one moment: no fear.

choke hold

The Saturday before Advent, we go to church for the family Advent gathering: pizza, a short worship service, and a chance to make our Advent wreath. As we walk to church, we bump into Carrie and her girls. Jack and Jane and Macy and Ava run ahead. Doug, carrying Luke, walks briskly after them. Holding Ben, I walk behind with Carrie.

"Do you remember meeting my friend Anna?" Carrie asks me. "The doctor with twins?"

I nod. I have a vague memory of a petite Asian woman introducing herself to me one evening at Carrie's house, while I sat on the sofa and lactated.

Carrie has tears in her eyes as she says, "One of her twins just got diagnosed with a brain tumor."

I feel like I've been kicked in the stomach. I clutch Ben to my chest. I try to breathe. "Oh Carrie." I can barely get the words out. "I'm so sorry."

She gives me a side-hug around my shoulders. "Me, too. He had surgery almost right away, and they got the tumor out, but he has to have six weeks of radiation in L.A."

Anna and her family don't live in L.A. Carrie tells me about the way Anna's December just rearranged itself around her sick son. I hold Ben close and fight tears. I don't understand how such things can be in a world created by a loving God.

***

Later, over pizza in the Fellowship Hall, I mention to Carrie the tingling in my feet that started three days ago, on Thanksgiving. She's a doctor. She might be able to help me.

"There's really only one thing to worry about," she says, "and that's Guillain-Barre Syndrome."

I don't know what Guillain-Barre Syndrome is, except that it's mentioned on all the vaccination release forms I have to sign whenever the kids get their shots. I decide I don't want to know what it is. I decide I should not have asked Carrie about this. I decide that I will not go home and google Guillain-Barre. I know that as soon as I read about the symptoms I'll start having every single one of them.

"Mostly, though," Carrie is saying, "you need to be sure you have feeling in your limbs. If you start tripping over your toes or you can't feel your fingers, that's when you should start worrying."

It's too late. I'm already worrying. *Worry* doesn't even begin to describe it. It's more like some demon has me in a choke hold. I can't finish my pizza. I go to the sanctuary and try to swallow.

Advent
the darkness deepens
(december)

My heart is in anguish within me
       The terrors of death have fallen upon me.

Thou knowest all our weeping, fainting, striving;
Thou know'st how very hard it is *to be*;
How hard to rouse faint will not yet reviving;
To do the pure thing, trusting all to thee;
To hold thou art there, for all no face we see;
How hard to think, through cold and dark and dearth,
That thou art nearer now than when eye-seen on earth.

—George MacDonald, *Diary of an Old Soul*

week one
waiting

I sit in the third pew on the pulpit side of the sanctuary. Jim reads the sermon text from Isaiah 9. As he reads, verse two catches me by the scruff of the neck and jerks my head up, as if to say, *listen up! These words are for you*:

> *The people who walked in darkness*
> *have seen a great light;*
> *those who lived in a land of deep darkness—*
> *on them light has shined.*

I feel like the people walking in deep darkness. I need that light to shine in my weary walking in a fog of sleep-deprivation and fear.

"God's solution to evil," Jim says, "is a baby who contains and embodies all the evil-defeating power of the heavenly hosts."

I pray that evil-defeating power over Michaela this morning. I pray that Wednesday's procedure will show that, despite her continued infections, the cancer has indeed been eradicated from her bone marrow. I pray it here in this pew, hard, my heart constricted with fear and trembling.

Jim declares, "We have a Heavenly Father who draws us home, who will do all that it takes to find us and bring us home. Each of us—*each of us*—is a beloved child of God, a creature of unimaginable worth and dignity. This Advent, let us allow the Father-Mother love of God to find us in whatever corner we're hiding in, in our fear that He is not safe or trustworthy."

I sit in the pew, stunned.

Those words were spoken just for me. God's light shining in the darkness of my fear—because Jesus knows I'm scared. Scared for Michaela, scared for my friend Lynne who has been ill all fall and still has no diagnosis, scared for Carrie's friend's son, scared, I admit, scared most of all for myself.

Last night, when I woke up just after midnight, every nerve in my body—arms, legs, hands, feet, face, back, belly—burned like so many wicks aflame. I remembered Carrie's words over dinner yesterday, and I was sure I had Guillain-Barre syndrome. Then Luke started to cry, and I found I could move. I could get out of bed. I could walk. I could pick him up and hold him. I still tingled like a star, but I could do what I needed to do. This morning when I woke up, the burning was gone from all but my hands and feet. So maybe it wasn't Guillain-Barre after all. Maybe I have MS.

As I nursed the babies in the church nursery this morning between services, Susan saw me and came in. I told her about the tingling.

She laughed at me. "Let me guess. You thought you had MS."

I laughed, too, but sitting here in the third pew, I'm still afraid. I need God to find me in this corner of myself in which I'm hiding because I am afraid He is not safe or trustworthy, because I am afraid, oh God, I am afraid He simply *isn't*.

***

Wednesday morning I feel sick with anxiety. I tell myself it's because Michaela's test is this morning. Jack, Jane, and I sit on the sofa and we pray for Michaela. Jane prays, "Thank you, God, for healing Michaela." Oh, that I had her faith. I force myself to breathe deeply and I invoke Psalm 63 and I beg God to hold me fast. Then I read *One Wintry Night* to Jack and Jane and breastfeed the babies and eagerly wait for Tiffany's text, which will either relieve my anxiety or send me into a paroxysm of tears.

"Good news!" The words pop up on my phone's screen, and I weep with relief.

"What's wrong, Mama?" Jane asks.

I shake my head. "Nothing. Nothing's wrong. Miss Tiffany just texted to let me know that Michaela's okay. The cancer is gone."

Jane smiles and hugs me. Jack says, "Mama, that's God's Advent present to us, that Michaela is better."

"Yes," I say through my tears and pull him into my arms. Yes. Yes. Yes. I am so grateful. Thank you, thank you, thank you, Jesus.

But despite Tiffany's text, despite this good news, the anxiety still chokes me.

grace notes, december 6

Doug makes breakfast this morning—he makes breakfast every morning—so I can get an extra half hour of sleep.

Doug's parents are coming today. They faithfully drive down every Monday to help me with the kids. And every Monday my mother-in-law sweeps my always-dirty floors.

A walk through the neighborhood with just Jack this afternoon. We scuffle through fallen ginkgo leaves on the sidewalk. Treetops with only a few leaves dance in sharply silhouetted relief against the dusky sky.

Ben's big grins that light up his whole face. Heck, they light up the whole room.

Luke's jerky happy kicks. He does the same jerky motions with his arms, but I don't know what to call them—punches?

Snuggling with Jane at bedtime. Her hugs are life-giving.

A quiet moment outside after dark, with the wind in my face, and my face toward the sky, and the sky partly cloudy, partly lit by stars and the waning gibbous moon.

week two
weary

Jim is preaching on Isaiah 9 again. He says, "The issue is always trust. Will we trust God?"

He says, "God's strength is made perfect in weakness."

He says, "Nothing, no place, no situation, is outside the authority of Christ's love."

I sit in the third pew. I am a dry and weary land. I am anxious and afraid, and I suck down his words like water in a desert. As his litany of trust goes on—Light shines in the darkness! The darkness cannot overcome it! The love of Christ is the final word! God is with us!—I try to breathe those words deep into my frightened heart.

Oh, Jesus, I pray as Jim's words wash over me, watering my soul, *help me to trust you. I am scared, Lord, scared of all that could go wrong in my life. Help me! Cast out this fear with your perfect love! Set me free! Give me joy! Give me peace! Thank you that I am growing in the midst of this—but oh, Jesus, does the growing have to be so painful? Is there no easier way to learn to trust you?*

And even as I pray those words, I know that this is the easy way. It does not feel easy, but it could be so much harder. I could be Tiffany, my daughter fighting cancer in her blood. I could be Carrie's friend, my son facing radiation. I could be Lynne, chronically exhausted and unable to find a diagnosis.

I am fighting fear, Lord, and it is real. But it is also only fear, and Your love casts it out, and I cling to You and Your right hand holds me fast. Hold me fast, Jesus. Hold me fast. I pray these words like a mantra, like a magic spell to keep the fear at bay. But nothing can keep the fear at bay. I pray the words anyway and weep my way through communion, through the songs that I can't sing for the tears in my throat.

***

Monday night, the boys sleep nine hours.

I do not. I wake up puking at one a.m. The only night in six months that I could sleep a normal, healthy amount, and I miss it.

***

My feet and my hands continue to tingle, so I email my doc, and she replies that I'm likely compressing a nerve or two from sitting in the same position for hours on end to breastfeed. Rationally, this make sense.

But I am too tired to be rational. I think I am dying. The tingling is the onset of some heretofore undocumented disease that leads quickly and inexorably to death. Every time I notice my feet tingling, I have a panic attack.

So much for not being afraid.

***

During tummy time, Luke reaches for and grabs a stuffed toy bug. I manage a smile, but Jack and Jane cheer for him. The winner of an Olympic medal could not have a more excited or enthusiastic audience: they jump and yell and wahoo and pump their little fists in the air. Watching them, my smile widens, deepens, becomes real.

***

Doug and I sit in the dark, silently, side by side on the sofa. He bottle-feeds Luke, and I nurse Ben. I stare out the window at our neighbor Mark's house, alight with color and white-light-swathed reindeer, and I am weary. I want nothing more than to climb in bed and sleep for a week.

"Come to me," Jesus says, "and I will give you rest." I want that rest.

In this Advent season of waiting, I am waiting for God's rest. I am clinging to the promise of Isaiah:

Those who wait for the Lord will renew their strength,
they will rise on wings like eagles,
they will run and not grow weary,
they will walk and be faint.

I want my strength renewed. I want those eagle's wings, and the stamina to run without flagging, to walk without fainting.

Ben sucks loudly, and I hold him a little tighter, remembering how Susan claimed this verse for him in those scary days when he was in the NICU at Children's, how she envisioned his battered, distressed lungs filling with the breath of the Spirit and his limp little body reviving and his strength renewing.

And I think: God did that. He did that for Ben.

And I think: God will do that for me, too. He will renew my strength. He will make my spirit soar. He will strengthen me and help me. He will uphold me with His hand.

He will. But He hasn't yet.

And I think: how apropos that it's Advent when I'm waiting for the fulfillment of promise. I know that Christ has already come, that God is my strength, right now, already. I know this, in my head. But that truth seems far removed from the place I'm living. Here, in the exhaustion and the bottles and the endlessness of laundry and dishes and diapers and dirty floors and failing books, God seems far off, and I am waiting for Christ to come.

The lights on Mark's house suddenly go off, and the darkness is, for a moment, total. Then my eyes adjust and I can make out the shapes of the sideboard, the piano, the dining room table, the baby in my arms, Doug beside me on the sofa.

week three
one more thing

Sunday morning, as I'm crossing the Fellowship Hall, I run into Tom. "Nine more days!" he calls to me.

"Hallelujah!" I say. The darkness has lain heavy upon us both this fall, and we are counting the days till the return of the light.

He grins. "So, when are you coming back to home group? We missed you again on Thursday."

I give him a weak smile. "Maybe in January?" I say. "Maybe by then the twins will be sleeping better, and I'll have energy for going out again."

"I don't know, Kimberlee," Tom says, laughing. "You're going to have four kids for a long time."

Panic washes over me in a giant wave. I force myself to laugh with him, then excuse myself. "I better scoot," I say, "or I'll be late for service."

As I walk away, the panic drains into my arms and legs. Tom's comment dashes cold water on my hope for a less exhausted future. Until this moment, I haven't thought much beyond getting through this current difficult stage. All of a sudden, I am no longer sure that more sleep will mean a better life. All of a sudden, the future looks like now.

My life is always going to be like this, with me on the knife-edge of okay.

No wonder I've been so anxious about my health and the babies' health and the kids' health and Doug's safety while biking to and from work each day: if I'm this close to the edge when everything is okay, what would I do if another ball got thrown at me? I'd drop them all. I'd fall apart. I'm already falling apart. I'd implode.

As I slip into the third pew, it dawns on me, all the things that have been thrown at me that I've absorbed these past months, big things like persevering through all that nipple pain so that I could nurse the twins and small things like mold all up the wall of our bedroom behind the babies' clothing bins. That hardly fazed me. I asked someone what to do and then took care of it. I wasted no emotional energy on it. Nor did I waste energy on the water in the basement when it rained super hard and streams of dirty water flowed all across the basement floor. I didn't even bat an eye at the ruined suitcases that the mice had peed in. Doug was grossed out and angry. I calmly threw the suitcases into the garbage can—zero emotional output.

I look at the purple banners proclaiming that the Word became flesh, that my soul glorifies the Lord, and I do. I glorify the Lord, even through my fear and the anxiety that courses through my veins. I glorify God for the ways He's transformed me. Seven years ago, when Jack was a baby, any one of those things would have done me in—crying, screaming, self-loathing, lying-on-the-floor-sobbing fits would have followed even one of them. I shudder to think what I would have done had all three occurred in less than three weeks, as they did this month. Even a year ago I would have been frustrated and angry. This year, I just shrugged, dealt with it, and moved on. I'd say that's a sign of growth, a sign that I'm learning what's important and what's not.

Which should encourage me to have hope for my future: God is at work on me and in me, and I will be okay.

I will.

Right?

***

Monday afternoon, and it's already dark out. Luke is asleep on his grandfather's chest—Grandpa is zonked out, too. Peggy sits beside them on the sofa and holds Ben, who is starting to fuss.

I stand in the kitchen, leaning over Jack and Jane, who stand on chairs at the counter. Jane is using a fork to lightly beat two eggs in a dish.

Jack reads the next ingredient from the cornbread recipe. "Two-thirds cup buttermilk." He opens the refrigerator and gets the buttermilk.

While he pours it, I make a well in the middle of the dry ingredients, which the kids have already measured into the bowl. "Okay, Jane, pour the eggs in." I point at the center of the bowl. She dumps in the eggs. Jack pours in the milk.

If my life were a movie, the camera would pan back from this idyllic picture of domestic bliss to show that the tomatoes on the stove have sloshed over the side of the pan and are even now being encrusted onto the heating elements; the sink is piled with dishes; the dining room table is covered with mail, crayons, scissors, and little scraps of paper; an overflowing basket of clothes sits in the living room waiting to be folded; my mother-in-law is holding a hungry baby who gets fussier by the second; and my anxiety level is ratcheting up.

There is not enough of me.

I say, "Just a second, Ben," as I wash a dish while the kids stir the milk and eggs into the dry ingredients.

"Just a second, Ben," as I pour the cornbread batter into a baking dish

"Almost there, Ben," as I wipe down the counter.

"Just have to drink this, Ben," as I down a glass of water—why am I so thirsty?

"Just one more thing, Ben," as I pour cooked tomatoes into the crock pot with the beans that have been cooking all day.

"Just a sec, dude. I know you're hungry," as I look at the baked-on tomato goo on the stovetop and I really have to clean it now because otherwise I won't get to it and it will still be there next week and then it will really be a pain to try to clean up.

He's wailing now. I look at him, see his little face bunched up in anger, his little mouth open wide as he screams. But I have to go to the bathroom. That boy might nurse for 30 minutes, and my bladder won't last that long. I say, "Honey, this time I mean it. I just have to do one more thing."

The bathroom floor desperately needs mopping. The laundry basket by the changing table is overflowing. The cats have tracked dirt onto the sink. Washcloths in various stages of drying hang from the shower curtain rod, lie over the bathtub rim, hang on the heat register. Flecks of pink mold color the grout in the bath surround.

Ben wails. Maybe I could at least pick up the washcloths? Ben's wail continues. He doesn't even pause for breath. He's that mad.

I resist the urge to do one more thing. Instead, I wash my hands and leave the mess and the bathroom.

"Okay, dude," I say to Ben. I scoop him into my arms and take him to the bedroom and feed him.

The instant silence makes me wonder: why do I feel compelled to do one *more* thing, instead of doing the one *needful* thing?

But I know the answer. I have to keep moving so the anxiety doesn't kill me.

***

Wednesday morning, Jane sits on the sofa, rocking a fussy Ben and singing "Away in a Manger" to him. When she gets to the line, "The little Lord Jesus lay down his sweet head," she stops singing and says to Ben, "Why don't you lay down your sweet head?"

From where I stand in the kitchen, I hear her, and I laugh. Grace, that.

***

I feel like I'm going to completely fall apart, so on Thursday morning I call Susan. I call Carrie. I call Laura. I call my mom. No one's home.

I want to call Tiffany, but she has far more reason for fear than I do, and I feel like a total jerk calling her up to cry about how scared I am that I have cancer when her daughter actually does.

I call my sister, and when she answers, I hole myself in my bedroom and cry into the phone. I tell her about the tingling. I tell her I think I have MS or maybe Guillain-Barre Syndrome. I tell her I'm so scared I'm going to die. "And then Doug is going to get remarried, and some stranger is going to raise my children." I sob.

Jen is silent a moment. Then she says, gently, "But Birdie, that can't happen till you die, and you're not dead."

I stop mid-sob. She's right. I'm not dead. I honestly hadn't even thought of that. I laugh through my tears. "Oh, Jen, how did I get to this place? How did I get so completely mental? I feel like a total nutcase, you know? Like an idiot. I know I'm being irrational—I'm not that far gone, thank God—but I'm too far gone to *stop* being irrational."

"Birdie," she says softly, "you're tired. You're exhausted. That's all it is. That's everything."

"Oh, Jen." I cry into the phone some more. Finally the tears run out. "Sissy," I whisper, too spent to even find my voice. "I'm so tired."

"I know," she croons. "I know."

week four
christmas at the solstice

The fear grips hard. Again. I count my blessings—that sacrifice of thanksgiving is what keeps me okay, barely, what gets me through the fear. I get up and do something. Wash dishes. Fold laundry. Chop an onion for dinner.

When I'm nursing and can't get up, I read to the kids. I read to myself. I pray Psalm 63 or memorize another verse of Ephesians. I write down another moment of grace or beauty or hilarity that I don't want to lose hold of.

In my best moments, I know that all will be well, that this present suffering will be transformed, redeemed, that God's in His heaven and all's right with the world.

But I am not living out of my best self these days; I am living out of my scared self. I am living in a place of existential darkness and it frightens me. "Yea though I walk through the valley of the shadow of death, I will fear no evil, for You are with me." Part of me thinks that's not nearly enough. My best self—the person I want to be—knows that it is, knows that Jesus is real and true and good, knows that Jesus knows how hard this is for me, knows that He carries me.

This morning Jack made up a new line for the worship song I often sing. "I will lift my eyes to the Shepherd, who always keeps me safe." Out of the mouths of babes.

The Shepherd leads me safely through dark valleys, even through death, to Life. This I believe. Oh help my unbelief.

***

The babies are sleeping. Jack is unloading the dishwasher. Jane is over at Carrie's, playing with Ava. Christmas carols blare on the stereo. The heater blasts warm air on this chilly day. Life is good. Very good.

And yet—I fear.

Jesus, fill me with Your perfect love. Cast out my fear. Heal me! I choose to believe, Lord, even though part of me fears You are not. Strengthen my faith, Lord. Help my unbelief, cast out my fear!

I see glimpses of God at work, at play all over my life—and yet the insidious voice of doubt whispers to my heart that perhaps it is all just a coincidence, that God is not Real.

I refuse to believe that. I can't believe that. Because that would mean this life is all there is, and once our loved ones die there is no hope of seeing them again. And how can I live without that hope? I can't. It's too painful, too horrible. It would be better never to be born than to love and lose and have no hope of reunion. Too many people have had lives that were too brief or too devoid of love or joy for me to believe that this life is it.

On the iPod, Amy Grant sings, "Surely you and I will find / Emmanuel, God with us."

I believe this, Jesus; help my unbelief.

Life is precious, each moment a gift, and my best self—the self that I long to live out of all the time—believes that God holds each moment, eternally present before Him, and when we stand before Him face to face, we will get those moments back, purified and perfected. We will. And if we don't, God will have something even better for us—something more than all we can ask or imagine.

I believe. Oh help my unbelief.

Oh Jesus, cast out my fear.

***

On the solstice, as soon as daylight dawns, Tom calls. The darkness has weighed heavily upon us both this fall, and we've been counting down the days till the return of the light.

"We made it," he says. "180 days of pure joy lie before us."

I smile into the phone.

I think—I am cautiously hopeful—that I'm coming back from wherever it is I've been this past month. I'm not exactly sure where I was or why I went there, but I'm pretty sure postpartum hormones and six months of sleep deprivation had something to do with it. And I'm very sure I don't ever want to go there again.

It was dark, and scary, sort of like an alley in a seedy part of town at two in the morning, with overflowing dumpsters, sticky sidewalks, and creepy shadows, a place where you're either going to slip in a giant pile of doggy doo and fall and crack your pate, or a thug is going to jump out of those creepy shadows and hold you up at knife point unless you turn over all your money only you don't have any because you suddenly realize you're standing there in the damp cold wearing nothing but your *chones*.

Except that makes it sound like it's almost funny, a comic version of fear.

And it didn't feel funny, though when I look back on it, I'm not sure why. It's not like anything about my life is different now, or was different a month ago before I went to hoodoo-land. Maybe that's why it's so frightening: because nothing was different, and at the same time everything was different; reality was suffused with fear, and no amount of deep breathing, positive self-talk, cognitive-behavioral therapy, or even prayer changed that. I felt alone in the alley of the shadow of death.

Madeleine L'Engle wrote frankly in several of her books about going through periods of atheism. I never understood that. I'm not sure I understand even now, but I definitely have been in a place of frightening agnosticism these past weeks, praying ridiculous and illogical prayers like, "Jesus, please be real" over and over again. For someone who wants her life to revolve around Christ, it's terrifying to think that the center may not be a Person but a black hole.

This morning, Tom's call is a flicker of light in the darkness that engulfs me. And as I smile into the phone, I am grateful not to be standing on the edge of the black abyss today. I am grateful that I've only had moments of looking over the edge into the darkness this whole past week. I am even grateful that when I was on the brink, I had the courage to look, to face the darkness and the fear, and to believe—oh, help my unbelief—that there is Light in the darkness, even if I couldn't see it. And I am grateful for Tom's phone call that is so completely not just a phone call—it's a glimmer of the joy that he proclaims to me. I stand here and grin into the phone, and for this blessed moment on this darkest day of the year, I believe with my heart and not just my lips that Tom is right, that the Light is coming—indeed, has already come—blazing into the darkness.

Christmas
hard to believe
(december/january)

Do not fear; only believe.

–Jesus, *The Gospel of Mark*

christmas eve

Everyone else is asleep. I should be sleeping, too. But I just need a few moments alone here at the end of the day. The lights on the Christmas tree are the only light in the house, bright enough to write by. They wink at me from across the room, cheerful red and yellow and blue and green. I wish I felt like winking back. I wish they made me feel cheerful.

I'm still holding fear at bay. It hovers around the edges of my life, but at least I am not so emotionally on edge these past few days, since Tom's call on the solstice: light will return, is even now returning.

Still, life feels very fragile. I feel very fragile.

The walls between me and the rest of the world feel so thin. The way my heart aches for Carrie's friend's son makes no sense; I've never even met the boy, only met Anna once, and briefly at that, long enough for a handshake and an exchanged "nice to meet you." And yet, this boy could be my son; my heart hurts that much. I feel so afraid for him. And for Michaela, who remains in and out of the hospital with infection after infection in her little bloodless body. And for Lynne, who might have MS.

In the face of such overwhelming fragility, I don't know how to pray for things like my book to sell so it won't go out of print. I'm trying to trust that God can hear my prayers for Michaela's healing, for Anna's son, for Lynne as well as my pitiful, selfish prayers for my book to remain in print—and honor both.

I look up at the Christmas tree, and I lay my concerns, my fears, my desires for myself, my family, my friends at Jesus' feet. And I will keep laying them down over and over again until they stay there, until life does not feel so hard.

Yes, I confess, my absolutely amazing and beautiful life feels hard right now. But I have infant twins; it's going to be a struggle, a challenge, and I will have days.

But I will also celebrate and rejoice and enjoy this good life I have, and I will hold on to hope and faith, even if I have to plead in tears before the throne of grace for the wherewithal to believe. I will learn that how I feel does not determine reality. It sure colors my perception of reality, but it does not alter what is Real and True.

That has been a huge grace in these past weeks: simply trusting—choosing to believe—that God is, even when I fear that He is not; and taking my fear to Jesus, who knows how it feels to hurt, to be afraid, to be abandoned even. To be able to pray, to be able to cling to God in the midst of my fear and doubt—that is God's grace to me, God's incarnation in my small, scared soul on this Christmas eve.

The lights wink their colors at me. *Hold me fast, Jesus, hold me fast because I keep losing my grip on You.*

christmas morning, 5 a.m.

Ben woke up at 3:30, crying, and would not be consoled. Then Luke woke up, and Ben was like, "Awesome, I woke up my bro," and zonked out. Luke, on the other hand, is still crying an hour later.

I walk around the dark living room, holding this wailing baby and weeping myself. I miss my life a year ago, when it was just the four of us. Desperately. I desperately miss life with two kids. Parenting four children looks very different than parenting two. I'm not able to give as much attention to each child as I'd like. The boys don't know any different, but Jack and Jane do. I ache for them. It's bad enough to grieve, but then you add the guilt of my half-wishing we'd never had the twins and how cheated I feel that I'm not getting to enjoy their baby-hood, and you get a very weepy, irritable, anxious Kimberlee. I'm tired of being weepy and irritable and anxious. I'm tired of being tired. I'm tired, period.

Luke finally stops crying. I collapse onto the sofa, him on my chest, and realize it's Christmas.

Joy to the world.

christmas night, 9 p.m.

I have sunk to a new low. I didn't even make Christmas dinner. We ordered pizza.

This morning, I built Lego castles with Jack and played Polly Pockets with Jane. Susan came over and broke out her record player, and we listened to the Mormon Tabernacle Choir sing Christmas carols. She watched the kids here at the house while Doug and I went for a brisk walk. Moving my body felt so good. Breathing outdoor air felt so good. And while we were gone, Susan cleaned the kitchen, God bless her.

The kids are sleeping now, and I am sitting here in the dark, looking at the candlelit crèche. As of last night, Baby Jesus is in the manger, with an adoring Mary looking down at him. I know how she feels. I love my kids, too. So much. And still I yell at them. Still I am impatient. Still I forget to hand out consequences calmly and with empathy, to solicit their good intentions. They want to be good; they want to please me; they just forget in the pleasure or excitement or irritation of the moment. And in my frustration, I forget, too, forget how much I love them, forget who it is I want to be, forget that I am shaping the direction of their lives, their characters, their souls by the words I speak.

Oh, Mary, didn't Jesus ever make you raise your voice in frustration, maybe even yell? Even once?

She's ignoring me, all her attention locked on her little boy in swaddling clothes.

Why couldn't she be the patron saint of mothers who want to be writers? Mothers who yell at their kids? Mothers who are weepy and anxious and afraid?

Maybe she is. She watched her beloved son die a criminal's death, publicly humiliated and scorned. I think that maybe she gets it, after all.

Maybe there's room in her mother's heart for her son's weepy mess of a disciple. Maybe I could lean my head on her breast, just for a bit, and be held.

A tear courses down my cheek.

I miss my mama. I just want someone to hold me and tell me everything will be okay. I just want to believe that.

the first sunday of christmas

The boys slept eight hours last night. I didn't even enjoy it: I kept waking up anxious and afraid, certain I was developing a chronic condition. A fatal one. Like lupis or MS or meningitis. So stupid. Such a waste of time and energy.

I tell Doug over tea that my arms ache and burn. "But it's a cold burn," I say, "like Icy-Hot or Ben-Gay. Only inside."

He nods, takes a sip of tea, and says, "It's probably arm cancer. I hear there's an epidemic of that going around."

I blink. "Really?"

He looks at me, hard. "You're kidding."

"Yes." I manage a weak smile. "Mostly."

"Our lives are good." He reaches over to place his hand on my forearm.

"I know." I almost wail the words. "I know. That's why I'm so freaked out. I'm barely okay with life being so good. What will I do if something awful happens?"

He squeezes my arm and smiles at me. "So you're creating things to worry about?" His voice turns gently teasing. "How is that helpful?"

He's right, of course. On both counts: I'm creating things to worry about and it's totally not helpful. Two months ago, I was freaking out over my milk supply, which is clearly fine. But I needed something to blame for this anxiety that's filling my body with its icy tingling fingers. Now that my milk isn't in any danger, I need something else to blame. Why can't I just blame the sleep-deprivation and the fact that I'm nursing two babies and have no appetite and can't get enough calories in my body, as Susan is constantly reminding me? Why do I always go straight to hypochondriac hell?

Doug and I get dressed, we get the twins dressed and help Jane find her shoes and Jack his jacket, and it takes 45 minutes just to get everyone out the door, but finally we all pile into the sofamobile. At church, when I see Susan, I tell her my arms feel weak and shaky. "It's a blood sugar issue," she tells me of my shaky limbs. "What have you eaten today?"

"Two biscuits with Nutella and an egg. And three cups of tea."

"Oh for heaven's sake, Kimberlee. That's like 150 calories. You're feeding two babies. You need to eat four times that much for breakfast."

But I have no appetite. The anxiety lives in my chest and stomach, sitting there like a boulder and leaving no room for food.

I sit in the sanctuary, in my customary third pew, nursing Luke and wishing I could stop the anxiety, could just decide not to feel anxious any more. But I've tried. Over and over again. And to no avail. It just sits here, crushing me.

Renee is preaching this morning. She reads John 8: "Then Jesus said to the Jews who had believed in him, 'If you continue in my word, you are truly my disciples; and you will know the truth, and the truth will make you free.'"

She looks out at us and smiles. "The truth will set us free. And the truth is that God is with us. This is the promise of Christmas. This is the truth that gives us freedom. And that is why we can trust God in the midst of our pain and our limitations: because He is with us."

I am trying to trust and believe that. I am trying to trust God in the midst of this, trust that He is faithful and true and real. And I am trying to be faithful—trying to use my anxiety and fear as a call to prayer and scripture recitation. I am clinging to God with the small strength that is in me.

Renee says, "The circumstances of our lives cannot block the purposes of God in our lives, and God *will* work out those purposes. *This is our hope*—" she emphasizes those words, hard, and I write them down "—God is who He says He is, and He is Truth, and Truth sets us free. All our hope is in Christ. He is the Light of the world. He is the God who is with us. And He is the Truth who sets us free."

In my journal, I write it big, Renee's words that speak to my quaking heart: TRUST GOD
IN DIFFICULTY,
IN PAIN,
IN DOUBT.
I'm trying. Oh, God, I'm trying.

gratitude and grief

When my in-laws arrive to hang out with the kids on Monday afternoon, Susan and I head over to the Episcopal Book Store, and my gut flutters wildly with anxiety, and my arms feel weak and cold, like I have ice water instead of blood flowing through my veins, and I think I'm dying.

As we browse the icons, I tell Susan I think all my anxiety and fear about my health and the kids' health is a mask for what I'm really scared of: I'm scared it will always be like this—me putting Jack and Jane off so I can tend to the babies, me barking at them, me weeping, me being mentally ill. I'm so scared for them. I'm scared that all my crying and anxiousness is scaring them—or scarring them.

We wander down the aisle, Jesus and Mary and various saints staring at us from the shelves.

"I haven't let myself admit that this is hard for me," I tell Susan. "I haven't let myself say that my life sucks right now. I look at Tiffany and I think how much harder it could be, and then I force myself to quit griping and be grateful."

"Kimberlee," she says gently, "those two things aren't mutually exclusive. You can feel more than one thing at a time. You can be grateful and grieve. You can be grateful and angry."

Tears prick my eyes. I nod and turn away, lips trembling, to look at an icon. Jesus holding his hand in a sign of peace.

I don't feel peace. I feel fear. I feel sorrow. I feel angry that I feel those things in the midst of what is really a very good life. I pick up the icon.

Susan says, "You're still feeling the fear and the sadness, you know. You're just projecting them onto other things—onto your health, mostly—as a way of rationalizing how you're really feeling."

The tears spill down my cheeks. I am afraid my life is over, because of the cancer or the brain tumor or whatever. But even though I don't have those things—and when I'm rational, I know I don't—there's still a sense in which my life is over; I'll never get those golden days of last autumn back, of life with two kids and Michaela with no cancer and my book still in its hopeful infancy, and even if I did, they probably wouldn't be as golden as I remember.

My grief runs deep, slicing through my veins, and I tremble. I set the icon down. "I'm ready to go," I say. I feel sick.

Susan nods, squeezes my arm, and we leave.

sheets

Jane is asleep in our bed. Jack is reading *Prince Caspian* in his bed. And I am in the kitchen, washing out my breast pump parts, sloshing warm, soapy water over the bottles and flanges and tubes. As I rinse them and drop them onto the drying rack, I realize that I didn't cry today. I almost cried. But I didn't.

I think this is the first day in over a month that I haven't cried. That's a nice present for this fourth day of Christmas. The day Jack was baptized. The Feast of the Holy Innocents.

Michaela, Lord. Caleb. And every other child who is suffering this night, children whose names only You know. Oh, Jesus, have mercy. Have mercy on me.

The kitchen is still a mess from dinner, there are clothes piled on the sofa, waiting to be folded, and I can't even look at my floors. I just have to pretend like they don't exist, like I'm not crushing cracker crumbs and raisins underfoot when I cross the kitchen. I really should sweep and mop.

I take a deep breath. I *should* sweep, but I *need* to sleep. There will always be more to do than I have time for. That's okay. Do what I can. The rest can wait. Or fall through the cracks, but I will not be anxious about anything. I will present my requests in prayer with thanksgiving to God. Even little requests, like time enough to order new sheets for our bed. The old ones have ripped right through. Sort of like me.

soul food

Jane sits on the sofa and sings to Luke, her own little made-up melody and words, but oh! such words to gladden my grieving, anxious heart: "Jesus Christ is the Light of the world, who takes away our sadness."

Out of the mouths of babes. She speaks straight to my soul.

new year

I stand over the boys' crib patting their bums while they wail and whimper with exhaustion, and I cry from exhaustion, too. And anxiety. I've cried so much this week—largely because I'm so tired. So so so tired.

And I pat pat pat their bums and I weep and I sing the Taize chant that has become my naptime mantra these past months:

In the Lord I'll be ever thankful.
In the Lord I will rejoice.
Look to God, do not be afraid, lift up your voices.
The Lord is near.

The Lord is near. I sing it to my boys, but mostly to myself. I am thankful, so thankful, and it only makes me aware of how much I have to lose, how little I deserve my many blessings, how life is so unfair. I think of Tiffany, of Anna, of Lynne. And I think, who am I that that is not my life? And I find it hard to trust God because such things happen. And yet—God saved Ben. He healed Ben. He gave me back my son, this happy, grinny, kicky, lovely boy.

Tears drop onto my hand, onto Ben's little swaddled back. How do I hold those things in tension? The goodness of my life, the many gifts I have, and the fact that I still find my life so difficult? And the more sobering fact that it could easily be so much harder? And the horrible reality that even if my life is good, others' lives aren't good in the same way? Anna and Tiffany don't have the gift of healthy children. Laura doesn't have the gift of an amazing husband who makes her tea every morning. Susan doesn't have any husband at all. Why don't they have those gifts? Why do I?

My tears fall harder, and my heart feels like it's cracking right open and all the fear and unfairness and suffering is leaking out my eyes. And then, it fills my mouth, and I want to scream, but I can't—I'll wake my almost-sleeping babies, I'll scare Jack and Jane who are in the living room waiting for me to read to them—so it erupts in a silent scream of pain, anger, anguish, as if I could rid myself of those things simply by opening my mouth wide enough, by crying hard enough.

second sunday of christmas

During the sermon, God speaks to me once more through the mouth of a babe, this one a girl of six, and I write it in all caps and underline it in thick black ink, what Renee's daughter Kelly told her: Christmas tells us that <u>GOD IS ALWAYS WITH US</u>.

writing my way to (barely) okay

I sit in the café window and stare at my computer screen. I came here to work while my in-laws are with the kids at home. But I cannot focus. Part of me is still home with the kids, worried if they're okay.

I pick up my pen and open my journal. I write:

I hate this dark place of fear and near-unbelief. I hate it.

But I can see glimpses of grace. The sky is blue blue blue. The sun is bright. The ads on the radio have given way to a triumphal overture.

I write and write and write my way back to a place of okay. Not good. Just okay. And barely that. But I'll take barely okay. It's way better than not okay. I see that even in the midst of the darkness and fear and doubt, I am growing. Grace, that. I am not growing up and out. I am not flourishing. Hardly. But I think—I hope—my roots are growing deeper into the Rock. Every time the doubts assail me, hissing their insidious words of fear and doubt into my soul and I say, "I believe! Help my unbelief!" I am anchored more firmly to the Rock. If only I could just keep writing all the time, every moment of every day, my pen reminding me of what I know, or ought to know.

Then I would be okay.

in which I send an email

After all the kids are in bed, Doug insists that I email our doctor and tell her what's going on.

"You know she'll probably prescribe antidepressants, right?" I say. He nods.

"But I'm breastfeeding. What if the medication gets into my breast-milk? What if it causes neurological changes in them? Doug, I can't."

"Yes, you can. Kimberlee, this has gone on long enough. You're not sleeping at night even when you can, even when the boys sleep, because you're so anxious. You think that's not getting into your breastmilk?"

I cave. I am tired. Tired of fighting. Tired of being anxious and afraid. Tired of these waves of fear that crash through me and make me afraid that God does not exist.

"Email her," Doug says and hands me my laptop.

***

My doc calls the next morning. She asks me a bit more about my email, asks, "How often do you cry?"

"Every day."

A pause. "And do you ever feel like something catastrophic is about to happen? Like the other shoe is about to drop?"

"Yes," I say, my voice hoarse with unshed tears. "All the time."

"We need to get you on medication right away," she says.

"I'm breastfeeding," I say.

"You can take this medication while you're breastfeeding. Sertraline is what I give to all my nursing moms with depression. Only about 5% of the medicine—and it's a tiny dose to begin with—ends up in your breastmilk."

She explains that sertraline is an SSRI. "That stands for Selective Serotonin Reuptake Inhibitor, and what it does is prevent your body from reabsorbing serotonin. If you imagine that each neuron in your brain is like a little storage unit with a couple of parking spaces attached to it, then the serotonin and other neurotransmitters are like cars that park in those parking spaces, allowing the neurons to communicate. Sometimes, if there's enough of a given neurotransmitter in your system, the neuron will absorb it, taking it out of the parking spot and into the storage unit. Are you with me?"

"I think so," I say.

"Your body for some reason thinks you have enough serotonin, so it's storing what it thinks is excess. But you don't have enough. That's clear from what you're telling me about how much you cry and your high anxiety levels. What the SSRI does is park in those parking spaces where the serotonin would park. That prevents the neuron from pulling serotonin into storage, which means there's more of it circulating in your system, and that helps stabilize your emotions, so you don't feel so anxious."

I'm quiet, my foggy brain trying to process what she's saying.

"Look," she says, as if she can hear my worry, my uncertainty. "If you were diabetic, I'd give you insulin, because you wouldn't have enough of it in your body. Since you're depressed, I give you this, because you don't have enough serotonin in your body to function normally."

"Okay," I say, even though it isn't. Then, just because I have to know, "I just don't want these boys to have to take sertraline their entire lives because I started them on it early."

She laughs. "Don't worry. It doesn't work that way."

I'm unconvinced. She can't know if it works that way or not because no one has done longitudinal studies on kids whose moms took antidepressant meds while nursing them.

When I mention this, she says, "You're right. But there are short-term studies that show no adverse effects. And there have been numerous long-term studies on kids whose moms were depressed, and those are sobering. I see it as a much higher risk to let you go untreated than whatever small effects your babies may experience as a result."

I think guiltily of Jack. He's always been a protector, fiercely loyal, especially to me. I think of how he's been taking on more than he should, to help and protect me, how he apologizes when Jane makes me cry or when the babies make me cry. How he gets mad and calls them bad babies or socks his sister.

I have to get myself together so that he doesn't grow up thinking my well-being rests on his shoulders or that it's his responsibility to make sure his siblings don't upset me. That's my job. Only I haven't been doing it so well lately. It's dark in here and every time I think I'm returning to the light, the darkness closes in again.

I need help.

"I'm giving you a one-month supply," the doctor is saying. "If this works the way I expect it to, I'll give you another six months' worth. I want you to go down and get this filled today."

This wasn't the help I wanted. I wanted a miracle of healing, a big bang of anxiety-eradicating God-power to come into my life and blast the fear away.

But it looks like God has other plans.

Oh Jesus, is this the path I should walk?

Epiphany
the color of hope
(january/february)

Oh, let me live in thy realities,
Nor substitute my notions for thy facts,
Notion with notion making leagues and pacts;
They are to truth but as dream-deeds to acts,
And questioned, make me doubt of everything.
"Oh Lord, my God," my heart gets up and cries,
"Come thy own self, and with thee my faith bring."

—George MacDonald, *Diary of an Old Soul*

the gift of the magi

At breakfast, per the pharmacist's instructions, I take my first anti-depressant.

I also go outside with Jack and Jane, and we mark the lintel of our front doorframe with the letters C, M, and B, the traditional initials of the Magi who journeyed from far-off lands to worship the Christ Child.

It seems fitting, I suppose, that these two things should happen on the same day, on Epiphany. Like the Magi, I'm looking for Jesus, too: it's been dark inside my head, and I am longing for the Light.

And though I've been praying like mad for deliverance and healing, God has not waved the divine hand and poofed away my fear. Yesterday, when I told Tiffany I was starting antidepressants, she gently reminded me, "Sometimes God uses medicine to heal us." She should know. God has been using chemotherapy—which is way worse for a kid than sertraline in his breastmilk—to heal Michaela.

So I humbled myself and went to the pharmacy and picked up my prescription. Thirty tiny blue pills. It's hard to believe that something so small might actually lift some of these fears that are kicking me in the gut and darkening my mind.

In fact, I don't believe it.

I bet the Magi didn't believe this poor Jewish kid was their long-awaited King, either. I imagine they looked at one another and raised their eyebrows and muttered that surely they had the wrong address. But they'd come all that way, and there was the star, shining down on that little peasant hovel. So in an act of faith, they presented their gifts.

My journey isn't nearly so glamorous. But God seems to have led me here, to this place where the next step toward the light seems to be in the form of a little blue pill. So in an act of faith, I swallow one down with my egg and biscuit.

out of print

I go to bed early. That pill has made me so tired, I could have collapsed from exhaustion several times today, but now I lie here and I can't relax. My anxiety is giving me tingles. My whole upper body feels like it's on fire. The more fearful I get, the worse the tingling is, so I get up and load the dishwasher. It's 11 p.m., and I'm scrubbing pots, wiping down counters, keeping myself moving because it keeps the fear at bay, or at least helps the tingling to be less painful.

As I empty the dish rack and wipe down the counter under it, I see the letter.

When Doug got home from work tonight, he brought in the mail and handed me an envelope from my publisher. I looked at it and then at him and said sadly, "They're taking my book out of print."

"You haven't even opened it."

I didn't have to. I'd been waiting for this letter since I got my royalty statement in November. I think my publisher wanted to wait through Advent to see if book sales picked up any with the beginning of a new church year. Apparently they didn't.

I slit open the envelope, read the letter, and cried. Doug held me against his shoulder. Then I dried my eyes and finished making dinner.

Now, washcloth in hand, I pick up the letter and read it again. I feel sick. The tingling in my arms makes me certain I have a terminal condition. When I die, will my publisher be sorry they pulled my book out of print?

My body hurts. My heart aches. I'm so tired I feel like puking. I lean against the counter, my head over the sink, wait for the nausea to pass. These pills are supposed to make me feel better, not worse.

I see no way that I will ever be able to write another book, not one that anyone will publish. I feel hopeless, especially since I'm convinced I'm terminally ill. And even if I'm not, the bleak reality is that I am now the author of an out-of-print book. That's probably worse than being unpublished. What publisher will take a chance on someone who's failed already?

I bend down, open the door of the cabinet under the sink, and drop the letter into the recycle bin. It doesn't matter. None of it matters.

"Mama!" Jack calls from his bedroom. "Mama!" There is fear in his cry. He turns on the light.

"Jack!" I say, rushing in. "Turn it off!" I flick the switch down. I don't want Jane waking up, too.

"I'm scared," he says. "Mama, I'm scared. The dark. The ancient kings."

"Oh honey," I say and hug him. I don't know where these ancient kings came from, or even what they are exactly, but he and Jane are both afraid of them.

"I'm scared, Mama," he says against my shoulder. "Will you cuddle with me?"

I hold him tight for a moment before I lead him back to his bed and boost him up onto the top bunk. Then I crawl up beside him and wrap my arms around him. I'm scared, too. I'm scared of the dark. I'm scared of things that are probably just as imaginary as Jack's ancient kings.

I lie in his bed, my tingling arms around my frightened boy.

hard to believe

Sunday morning Julianne is helping at Godly Play. I manage a smile when I bring Jack up to the worship center. I sit with him on a carpet square and read *Does God Know How to Tie Shoes?* Julianne kneels in front of him. "Jack," she says, "are you ready to worship?"

He shakes his head. "I want Mama to finish the story first."

She nods and moves away, gathering the other children and ushering them one by one into the worship center. I read softly to Jack. When I close the book, all the other children are inside the worship center. Julianne leads Jack inside but motions me to stay for a moment. I wait for her.

She smiles as she comes back out. "How are you? Are you doing okay?"

I blink back the tears that swim right up into my eyes and shake my head. "I started taking antidepressants on Thursday," I tell her.

"Oh Kimberlee." She gives me a big hug. "I will keep praying for you."

I nod. "Please pray that..." I can barely speak for the tears that are thickening my throat. The tears brim over, and I choke out, "I'm so scared. It's hard to believe."

"Oh Kimberlee," she says again, her voice filled with understanding. Her arms around me tighten. "This depression is deep. Your faith is so central to you. It's the foundation of who you are."

I weep on her shoulder, and my heart takes courage from her words. That she would say such a thing, that she would *see* such a thing. That my faith is visible to others, that it is visible to Julianne, who is not in my circle of close friends, that she can see how deeply important it is to me—it makes me weep. It reminds me who I am, who I truly am—a woman of faith, deep faith—and reminds me that the truest thing about me is my Belovedness, my rooting and grounding in Jesus.

No wonder I'm scared. The very foundation of my identity is being shaken. I think this must be what is meant by a dark night of the soul. I've read about that, but until now I've never experienced it: this sense of hopelessness, this fear that everything I believe is not true. How can I live without faith? Without hope? And without Jesus, there is no hope, for there is no resurrection, and death is the end, and how can we comfort ourselves now?

We can't. There is no comfort. There is only death and oblivion awaiting us, awaiting our children, and I refuse to believe that. I can't believe it…because then I would live in this fear all my life, and this is no way to live. So I say, "Blessed be the name of the Lord." Because I want to be faithful. Because I want to believe that Light and Love and Life everlasting have the last word.

I dry my tears, sniff a little. Julianne hands me a tissue. "Thank you," I say softly. "Thank you." I'm not thanking her for the tissue.

She smiles, squeezes my arm, and slips into the worship center, while I head downstairs, clutching that tissue tight in my hand. I believe. Oh help my unbelief.

ice and fire

Monday, Doug's parents come down again. While they watch the kids, I go see Margie. She asks the question she always asks, "Where have you seen God these past weeks?"

And I cry. I tell her about the antidepressants and how hard it is to believe and how scared I am and how I've been trying everything—everything—to fight the fear and how none of it has worked and the medication seems to be making things worse. "I recite Scripture, and I pray all the time. I can't not pray; it's all that's getting me through. I keep taking grace notes. But it's not enough. It's not enough." I weep into my scarf. "I'm still scared all the time."

She sits with me in my fear and lets me cry.

When I'm a little calmer, she says softly, "My God, my God, why have you forsaken me?"

I look at her.

"That's how it feels." It's not a question.

"Yes." I nod. "But—can I say that?"

"Kimberlee," she almost laughs, "Jesus said it. Of course you can say it."

"But he was on a cross, Margie! He was suffering."

She is silent a moment. "And you think you're not?"

I stare at her. How can I possibly claim that? I have four healthy children, an amazingly supportive and loving husband, a warm house, a church community that's still bringing me meals after six months. "Margie," I say, "I have one of the best lives in the history of the planet." I pause and get teary again and choke up, and I say the next words softly. I feel ashamed. "It just doesn't feel like it."

She nods. "Because it's not. Kimberlee, your mental health is a part of your life. It's a part of *you*. With your brain chemistry all whacked out like this—no matter how many grace notes you take, you're still ill. And illness is a form of suffering. Even you'd say that."

I would.

We sit quietly while I ponder this. "So you think it's okay to say that? To ask God why He's abandoned me? Or why I feel like He has?"

She nods. "Absolutely."

***

That night, I can't stop crying. I feel completely out of control. I don't think I should be alone right now. I ask my in-laws to stay till Doug gets home.

Peggy sends me to bed. I lie staring up into the dark, listening to Peggy feed the babies, to Jack and his grandfather building a Lego airplane, to Jane singing to herself, and I am very, very afraid.

In tears, I call Susan. "I am so afraid," I tell her, weeping in the dark. "I'm afraid I'm going to kill myself."

She's calm. "Do you want to kill yourself?"

"No," I weep, "of course not. But Susan, I don't want to be anxious, either, and I can't control that. I haven't been able to control that for months! I feel so scared, like I might do something to harm myself, even though I don't want to. I feel like my mind isn't my own anymore."

"Kimberlee," her voice is firm, "you are not going to kill yourself. Your mind is your own. You just have a tendency to fixate on things and worry about them. Like cancer. Or MS. Or meningitis. This is the same thing. You read on the sertraline info sheet that it can cause some people to have suicidal thoughts, and you're freaking out."

If I weren't so beside myself, I'd laugh. If only I *were* myself, I'd laugh. Oh God, if only I could. But it's so completely not funny. It's terrifying. Susan talks to me until Doug gets home.

Through my tears, I whisper into his chest. "I'm afraid I might hurt myself."

He tips my head back and looks at me long. He smiles a small smile.

"I trust you, Kimberlee. I know you won't."

He and Susan have a whole lot more confidence in me than I have. I try to take comfort from this, try to tell myself they're right to trust me and I should trust myself, but I don't. I don't. This fear that's got me by the throat is unlike anything I've ever known. I can't fight it. I can't laugh at it. I can't beat it. It's beating me.

That night, my whole body tingles like it's on fire. The babies are sleeping in their crib. Doug is sleeping beside me. But I can't sleep. Again. *Again.* I didn't sleep much last night either.

Panic rolls over me in wave after wave, every wave a blast of ice running through my arms, my legs. Ice and fire. That's what it feels like. Fire in my nerves, ice in my veins. I am dying. I must be. And oh God what if You're not real? What if I never see my children again? I cry silently in the darkness, tears slipping down my temples into my ears, onto my pillow.

At four a.m., I get up and call the doctor. "I don't think these meds are working," I tell her voice mail. "I feel way worse than I did before. I can't sleep. I keep having panic attacks. Lots of them."

I sit on the sofa and stare out the dark window. Panic rolls over me in a wave. I can't take this. I can't take any more. I start to cry again. I don't want to wake anyone, so I go to the bathroom.

I leave the overhead lights off, and seeing by the little nightlight, the one with the cheerful fairies on it that I bought when Jack was born, I turn on the showerhead, wait for the water to warm. I step into the bathtub. I am so tired. So tired. I sit down in the bottom of the tub, my forehead resting on my arms, my arms resting on my knees. Water sprays down on me, drips down my hair, my back, and panic rolls inside me like waves over sand, constant and erosive, abrading all I think, all I believe, all I am. The fear is like fire in my veins; my arms burn with it. And I have no energy left to fight the unrelenting demons. I sit in the dark shower and sob and I know why people kill themselves. It takes too much effort to live, and I am so tired. I just want to lay me down, right here in the shower, right now, and sleep and never wake up, and oh God, what will happen to my kids if I do?

mercy, grace

Later that morning, my doc calls me back, asks how I'm doing, and I tell her I'm better. I tell her I'm tired, so tired, but for the first time in as long as I can remember, I am just tired.

I don't know what happened. I don't know if my medication suddenly kicked in after four days. Or if God finally said to the powers of darkness, "Enough!" But in the midst of the fire and ice and panic in my shower this morning—right in the midst of it—mercy. Grace. The fear subsided. The burning cooled. I sat there, water raining down on me, and for the first time in months, I sagged with exhaustion untainted by anxiety.

By the time my doc calls, I think I am going to be okay. I tell her I think the weakness in my arms is just a remnant of the anxiety, or a function of low blood sugar, or both, and that I probably need to eat something.

She says I sound like I've made a pretty accurate self-diagnosis and tells me to get off the phone and go eat a hamburger.

sleep training

A few days later my doc calls again and asks me how I'm doing with my new happy meds. It's been a week since I started taking them. She asks how I'm feeling.

"Tired," I say.

"How much are you sleeping?"

When I tell her I've slept ten hours in the past three nights, she's appalled. These drugs are, among other things, supposed to help me sleep.

I assure her it's not the little blue pills that are keeping me awake. "It's the babies. They've been up and up and up like newborns all week, wanting to eat every couple hours."

"Stop feeding them!" she says. "They're almost six months old! They can get through the night without food."

"But they wake up crying."

"So let them cry."

We do. That night they cry for three and a half hours. Finally, at five a.m., I give in and feed them, just to shut them up. After all that noise for so long, the silence is deafening.

Friday night is much, much better. They're only up a couple times each for about 20 minutes or so. Hooray for sleep training! This is going to be easier than we thought. I begin to dream of actually sleeping at night, all night. Oh bliss.

Or not. Saturday night, Luke cries for an hour. Sunday night, he cries for an hour and a half.

I think he's defective.

This is not the first time I've thought that. I can't decide if I want to send him back for a better model or just cut my losses and put him out on the curb with a free-to-good-home sign around his neck.

Doug informs me, "I think that's illegal. You'll end up in jail."

"Jail?" I think this over. "Would I have my own room?"

Ben, on the other hand, is a dream baby. The past two nights, when he's woken up, he's whimpered, maybe wailed once or twice, and then gone back to sleep.

This morning during tummy time, I lie down on the carpet beside him and say, out loud, in front of his brother, "Bennet, you are my favorite baby, you know that? You good little sleeper, you. That's right: you, young man, have officially achieved Favored Baby Status."

Jack chimes in with his annoying Aunt Petunia voice. "Dat's wight, Benno. You're Mama's ickle widdle favowite baby."

Luke is unconcerned. He just lies beside Ben on his tummy and sucks on his hands. I can't help it. I kiss his little bald head.

fading fast

The night that I asked my in-laws to stay till Doug got home because I didn't think I should be alone, Peggy called my mom. The next morning, right after my doc called, my mom rang up. "I just bought a ticket to Seattle," she said. "I'll be there for two weeks."

And here she is, swooping in like my guardian angel, washing the dishes, folding the laundry, sweeping and mopping my disgusting floors. My home hasn't looked this homey and undestroyed since she left in September.

The first Friday she's here, she sends me out at dusk for some fresh air. "You've been indoors all day. Go for a walk."

So I bundle up in my brown scarf and pink coat and step out into the crisp cold. The moment I turn the corner, I catch my breath: the sunset is beautiful. I chase it, trying to find ground high enough to be able to see it unobstructed. The closest I get is a three-foot-high curb in a church parking lot two blocks from our house.

But even the rooftops and power poles and electric lines poking up into the sky can't block the beauty. The whole southwestern sky is the color of ripe raspberries, a whole bowl of them, spilled out and illuminated, as if lit from behind, or within. I want to fly up to it and swim in it. I want to eat it.

Instead, I stand, earthbound and wide-eyed, in the church parking lot and watch that vibrant pink drain from the sky. It fades really fast.

Not an hour before, my mom and I had been looking at baby pictures of Jane. Mama shook her head and said, "I just don't remember Jane as a baby."

"I don't either," I said. "I didn't realize how much Luke looks like her." How could I look at Luke and not see the resemblance? How could I forget something so unforgettable as my only daughter's baby face?

My memory fades so fast, and the days fade even faster, and I know that tired as I am, I will likely have almost no memories of this first year of the boys' life, and that makes me sad. It makes me want to hold on. It makes me want to pay attention. The pink pales to a mere blush and then sinks into the west. Darkness descends. A star—or it might be Jupiter—winks down at me. I smile into the sky, then turn to head home.

When I open the front door, Jane runs to me, jumps into my arms, and hugs me. "I love you, Mama! I missed you!" I hold her close, smell her hair. She pulls away to look at me. Her cheeks dimple, and her blue eyes shine. I smile into her smiling face. I will miss the little girl she is. I already do. I want to pay attention. I want to be able to remember.

Because it fades really fast.

oh me of little faith

The house is quiet and dark. Mama sits beside me on the sofa, the only light the soft spill of the street lamp through the window at our backs. Luke is asleep on Mama's chest. Ben is asleep on mine. It is the perfect, idyllic moment. Or should be. But I have an anxiety attack as I sit here, and the fear returns, the fear that God is not.

"Oh Mama," I whisper, and tears come to my eyes. "I am so scared."

"Scared?" she says. "Of what?"

I can barely speak it, but I need her to know, want her to understand. "I'm scared God isn't real, that everything I believe isn't true."

"Oh, honey." She puts her hand on my arm. "After all that you've seen, all that you've lived—" she lays a hand on Ben's back "—how can you doubt?"

"I know," I whisper, and tears fall down my cheeks. "I know." I do know. And I don't.

six months and counting

The babies are six months old today.

I can hardly believe it's already been six months. I can hardly believe it's only been six months.

They're sleeping better at night. They're more interactive during the day—smiling, laughing, reaching for my hair and holding onto it for dear life. They've started solid food. And they have the poops to prove it. Pee-yew.

They've begun acknowledging each other's existence, which is a relief. For awhile there, I wondered if they were even aware that there were two of them. Last night, they were holding hands while I breastfed them. It was pretty darn sweet, sort of made up for the fact that I had two babies lying on my chest sucking the life out of me.

Last week, when I took Jane to Ava's birthday party, I met a dad of twins and two singletons—just like us. He appeared normal and healthy. He smiled. He laughed. I watched him and thought, *that is my future.* I talked to him and he said having four children was a blast. And, like so many other parents of twins, he told me the first six months are the hardest. Glory be! We're through the worst of it.

Of course, he also said the second six months are the next hardest. So maybe we're not through the worst quite yet.

Still, I try to console myself that we're halfway through the hardest year. I try to believe that it will only get better from here. After all, my meds seem to be working: I am no longer having panic attacks or dissolving on a daily basis into a blubbering mass of Mama-jello on the floor.

I try to remember that I now have whole hours in the course of a given day when I'm not anxious, when I think maybe I haven't ruined my life after all. Maybe that dad was right and having four children will be a blast. Maybe I'll figure out how to get dinner on the table at a reasonable hour. Maybe that will even happen before Jack leaves for college.

There are other hours in the day, though, and those aren't always quite so upbeat, hours in which I wonder if the best years of my life are behind me, or if this is as good as it gets, or if there is meaning to life. Luckily, those hours pass, and then I am more or less okay again.

Of course, okay is a relative term. My margins still feel really thin, like the least little thing could send me over the edge into not-okay.

Today, for instance, I cried two different times, for reasons I can no longer remember. My mom is still here, and all I could think was, *How have I done this without her? How will I do this without her?*

But I have, somehow. And I will again. After all, I've made it through the hardest months.

At least, that's what I keep telling myself.

grace notes, february 4

The way my mother sits, legs crossed, in the rocking chair, working a crossword puzzle.

The way my daughter's hair curls softly around her face as she sits beside me on the sofa, looking at a book. The dimple in her chin. The arch of her perfect eyebrows. Even the bug bites on her legs that she's picked till they've bled and scabbed over.

The way Ben plays with my fingers while he nurses. The cool softness of his cheeks. The soft down of his hair.

The way Luke shrieks with delight when he shakes the rattle he's managed to pick up. His chubby cheeks and chin. His Buddha belly.

The way Jack's hair falls across his forehead and over his ears. The small scar beside his nose. His joyful singing as he sits at the table, drawing.

This moment, right here, right now.

Even the way my heart aches with the fullness, the fleetingness, of it all.

the color of hope

I almost miss them.

On Saturday, we walk up to the park to play for a bit, and on the way home, we pass a tree in the planting strip: there, against a gray branch under a gray sky—three palest pink blossoms.

I am nearly past them before I see them. I stop walking. "Jack, Jane, look! Cherry blossoms!"

They look. They couldn't care less. It's much more fun to chase each other, screaming, down the sidewalk. So they do.

Doug smiles at me. "They're pretty," he says.

And they are. But it's more than that. It's that until this moment I had forgotten about cherry blossoms, forgotten how they start blooming in mid-January, forgotten that a month from now the trees will be covered in pink blossoms, forgotten the way their petals carpet the sidewalks, forgotten the way their beauty fills me year after year with such joy it almost hurts.

How could I forget that?

When I get home, I notice our camellia tree is thick with buds. After the cherry blossoms will come camellias. Then crocus. Then daffodils and tulips and iris.

Winter will pass. Spring will come. Light will lengthen.

I knew that, cognitively. But in the darkness of these past months, I had forgotten.

I finger a glossy green camellia leaf. How glad I am that I didn't miss those cherry blossoms, that they caught at the corner of my vision, that I turned my head and saw. "They're pretty," Doug said. But they were more than pretty.

They were the color of hope.

epiphany

After my conversation with Julianne the Sunday after Epiphany, she called a bunch of folks and arranged for another dozen dinners to be delivered to us this past month. Tonight, she brings dinner herself. As she unloads the bag of food she's brought, she asks me how I'm doing.

"Better," I say, "though it kind of freaks me out that a little blue pill can make me believe in God again."

She looks at me quizzically. "But, Kimberlee, you *already* believed in God."

I feel like the kitchen floor falls out from under me, so abruptly do her words strike me with the light of truth. She's exactly right, of course: I did already believe in God. All through that dark night, or whatever it was, I clung to God. Sometimes by my fingernails. Often with tears and trembling. But I kept calling on Jesus to come and save me. I kept taking grace notes and giving thanks for them—an act of faith that it was indeed God who was at work, even though my eyes felt so clouded I couldn't see. And I couldn't. It was dark, so dark that I had to grope my way forward by faith.

I remember what one of my grad school profs told us about Gregory of Nyssa's vision in *The Life of Moses*, how the mountain of Sinai grew so dark with the thick cloud of God's presence that Moses was blinded by it, how he had to press blindly forward into that infinitely brilliant darkness. One step of faith at a time, I expect.

The kitchen floor becomes solid under my feet again. I look at

Julianne, who's still smiling quizzically at me, and I smile back. "Yes," I say. "I did."

Even in my fear, I chose faith. Even in my unbelief, I believed.

Lent
the light lengthens
(march/april)

I will extol you, O Lord, for you have drawn me up,
   and did not let my foes rejoice over me.
O Lord my God, I cried to you for help,
   and you have healed me.
O Lord, you brought up my soul from Sheol;
   you restored me to life from among those gone down to the Pit.

—Psalm 30

ash wednesday

At the Ash Wednesday service, Jack and Jane receive their first communion.

I had intended their first communion to be a big deal. I'd wanted them to make a public profession of faith in Christ before they received their first communion. But this wasn't public or big. It was quiet, anticlimactic even, at least for me. But perhaps that is better. Drawing near to Jesus is not a public production but an inward movement of the heart.

Doug and I choose tonight because I remember how last year I felt wrong letting them receive the ashes, sign of our mortality, but not the bread and wine, symbol of our redemption and resurrection. The ashes are only half the story—less than half—and the sad and sorry half. The bread and wine allow us to live, with joy, in the midst of our pain and brokenness, in the face of death. We want Jack and Jane to experience the fullness of their story tonight, the wholeness of their life in Christ.

They walk forward with us, not with arms crossed upon their chests to receive a blessing, but with hands open to receive the body and blood of Christ.

hallelujah

I know it's Lent and I'm not supposed to say hallelujah. But I don't care. Break out the tambourines. Bang the bongos. Cue the Hallelujah Chorus.

The babies are sleeping through the night.

Last week, we moved them out of our room and into the kids' room. It might be the best parenting decision we've ever made. All of a sudden they started sleeping eight or nine hours a night.

Which means I'm sleeping eight or nine hours a night. (Oh joy, oh bliss, oh night divine.) Several people, upon hearing this marvelous news, have asked if I feel like a new woman.

Actually, not so much. I feel like a very, very tired woman. After three consecutive nights of good sleep, I'm more exhausted than I've been since I started living better through chemistry.

My doctor says it takes about two weeks of good sleep to feel immediate relief and two to three months of good sleep to fully recover. If this new turn of events continues (knock on wood), that means I'll be feeling like that new woman by the ides of March and be fully rested sometime during Easter. How perfect is that?

soft answer

It's 9:30 a.m., and I'm ready to go back to bed.

I've changed four poopy diapers already this morning. The babies wailed all through breakfast—Luke because I wasn't feeding him fast enough, Ben because I was trying to feed him at all. It took me half an hour to get a half-cup of oatmeal and pears into that child. I desperately need to shower. And I really want a nap.

I manage to get the babies down, and then Jane throws a fit when I ask her to pick up the Polly Pockets she's strewn all over the floor. So I pick them up and put them in toy time-out. This provokes another fit. When she asks if she can wear her new dress and I say she may wear it to church on Sunday but not today, she pitches a third fit.

I want to smack her, so I leave the room.

She and Jack start fighting—over a box. I take it away. She flops onto the floor in a huff. Jack drags his Lego bin into the living room, and I ask him to please take out the garbage before he gets out his Legos. He gets mad, slams his drawers when he goes to his room to get his socks and shoes, and wakes Luke up, because around here, everybody shares a room. When I reprimand him, he grabs Jane and squeezes her arm so hard she cries. Now I want to hit *him*.

I gather Jane in my arms and send Jack outside with the garbage. Then I go deal with Luke, who (thank the Lord) goes back to sleep.

When Jack comes back in, I remember—thank you, Jesus—to hug him. He's acting like a beast, and he needs to know I love him anyway.

So I kneel on the floor in front of him and ask, "Have you had a hug yet today?"

He shakes his head. "No."

"Well, come here," I say, and he does, and I wrap my arms around him.

"I love you, Mama," he says. He sits in my lap, and I hold him. We don't talk, just sit there.

"You okay now?" I ask after a bit.

He nods.

"We'll read stories as soon as you take out the recycling."

"Okay, Mama." And he walks to the kitchen and I am left sitting on the floor wondering if it's really that simple?

Maybe not always, but it sure worked today. I think of the verse the kids and I memorized back in September or October: "A soft answer turns away wrath." I always thought that meant that if I answered softly, I'd quell the wrath of the person who was mad at me. But apparently a soft answer also quells my own wrath because, amazingly, I'm not angry anymore. I'm still tired, and I still want a nap, but I think I just might have enough energy left in me to get through this day without screaming. That right there is a gift from God.

grace notes, march 11

Three nights of blessedly, gloriously uninterrupted sleep.

My red hoodie.

Moleskine journals and datebooks.

An article I wrote last year got accepted for publication—and they're paying me for it!

Those little blue pills that are bringing me back to myself.

Morning hugs from Jane.

Sunshine!

Jack's laugh.

Baby skin, so soft.

Paperwhites in bloom.

An email from Lynne; her symptoms seem to be resolving, and she has more energy than she's had in months. Thank you, God!

My dishwasher.

Hot tea soothing my sore throat.

12 pairs of baby socks from Doug's mom, who pitied the poor twin-
fants: they were down to one pair each.

Did I mention sunshine?!?

New-to-us books from the library.

Michaela is done with her year of intensive chemo!

The Jesus Prayer.

My rocking chair.

Doug, always.

box wall

On Wednesday, I decide to step out onto the porch and stand in the bitter cold and breathe fresh air and sunshine for a few minutes. But when I open the front door, I run into a wall of boxes. I can't even open the screen door far enough to squeeze outside.

There are 14 boxes sitting on my porch. Each box contains 72 books. Or rather, 72 copies of one book.

My book.

That's 1008 copies of my book that are sitting here on my porch. Two very generous friends gave me enough money to buy all these copies so they wouldn't get slashed and burned or whatever it is that happens to out-of-print books that no one wants.

I take one look at them, step back inside, and shut the door.

I don't open it again till Doug gets home. My first inkling that he's arrived is the shout of laughter I hear. Then I hear him hefting the boxes to the other side of the porch: he can't get to, let alone through, the barely-opening screen door. Once he gets the screen open, he conscripts Jack to help him carry the boxes into the living room and stack them there. The boxes take up most of the room.

After dinner and story time, while Doug tucks Jane in and Jack reads *The Voyage of the Dawn Treader*, I schlep the boxes down to the basement.

"Do you want some help?" Doug comes out of the kids' room to ask.

I shake my head. "Nope. I want to do this myself." But as I heft the seventh or eighth box into my arms, I think maybe that wasn't such a good decision. There's nothing quite like carrying fourteen 24-pound boxes of your own out-of-print book down concrete steps to a dimly lit cinder block room to engender a feeling of futility.

When the last box is in the basement, I come back upstairs and wonder aloud what I am going to do with all those books.

Doug suggests, "Maybe you should offer a free ginsu paring knife to anyone who buys two copies."

I grin at him. "Let the shilling begin."

green again

I thought I'd killed it. Lopped off both its ugly heads and left it lying dead.

I should have known better. The green-eyed monster is a Hydra: when you whack off its heads, it grows new ones. Sometimes that takes awhile, which is why I was lulled into believing I'd actually killed this beast.

But it's back, its ugly heads twisting up from my gut (or maybe they live in my heart?) and wrapping round my shoulders and hissing their sibilant words in my ears.

I tell Margie, "I am jealous as hell of Emily Barrett. Her newest book came out in January—and it's a *New York Times* bestseller."

It's not like I think she doesn't deserve it. She's been writing beautiful prose in relative obscurity for the better part of a decade. She deserves this if anyone does. But the green-eyed monster doesn't care about that. He just hisses in my ears how I'll never be like her, how her success takes away from the possibility of mine and I should hate her hate her hate her. I don't. Truly I don't. I'm kind of in awe of her. I am also green green green with envy.

Margie says, "It's actually an encouraging sign, Kimberlee, don't you think? That you have the energy to be envious."

I blink. "Now that's a depressing thought—that the primary sign of my returning mental equilibrium is the fact that I'm jealous of a fellow writer who's never been anything but kind to me—"

"You know her?" Margie asks.

I shake my head. "I've read all her books, so I feel like I know her. But I don't. Not really. We've had an email exchange—I emailed her last fall to thank her for her words and how much they'd help me weather the first few months with twins—and she wrote back. She said she was praying for me and for the boys. *Praying* for me, Margie."

I feel like a worm.

Anne Lamott calls the stereo effect of the green-eyed monster's voices "Radio Station KFKD." In one ear, you hear how lame you are, how you'll never amount to anything, how this other writer beat you to the publisher and has stolen your audience, how she'll always come out ahead and you'll always be behind and you can't write anyway and who are you kidding you aren't really an author your book is out of print.

In the other ear, you hear how unfair it all is, how you're at least as good a writer as that writer who stole your spot on the bestseller lists (and a good many others too) and she doesn't deserve the success she has and it's not your fault you can't afford a full-time nanny to care for your kids and a housekeeper to take care of your house and give you time to write and it's just not fair, poor sad tired tired sad sad you.

The truly icky thing about the green-eyed monster is that I don't know it's wrapped me in its horrible heads until it's too late, until the envy has started raging and I'm already mired in the self-loathing and the self-pity and there's part of me that just wants to give in and listen to those siren voices, listen and believe.

Margie says, "Your envy is trying to tell you something, Kimberlee. It's trying to tell you what you want." She gives me a gentle smile. "So, what is it that you want, do you think?"

I shake my head. "I don't know. I mean, when I really stop and think about what it would mean to have a bestselling book, I think it would suck. Not entirely. It'd be really giddy, too. But then you have all the pressure of writing another one and the fear that you can't and the very real possibility that your biggest success is behind you. No thanks. And then there's the fact that small-minded people like me will be thinking nasty things about you, and who needs that?" I shake my head. "When I think about those things—even just talking about them—my envy dies away."

"Okay," Margie says, "so if it's not the bestseller bit, what is it?"

I think for a few moments, staring out the window at the birch tree that's beginning to show green buds. "I think it's that her book is so beautiful. I mean, physically, it's beautiful to look at and to hold. And her writing—" I pause, trying to find words. "Her language is so rich and poetic, and her vision of the world is—sacramental. She sees Christ everywhere. That's part of it. I envy her vision. And I envy the way she writes. It's beautiful and evocative in ways that my writing never will be—because if I wrote like that, it'd just sound phony. But it's natural for her.

"And honestly? I'm jealous that she's been able to capture her readers' imaginations, to draw them into her life and win their affection. I'm jealous that her book is winning readers—lots of them—and mine is out of print." I scrunch up my nose. "Saying that out loud makes me feel very small-minded and ugly."

"Envy is only ugly if you let it best you," Margie says. "Otherwise, it can be a call to prayer, just like anything else."

"So you're saying that whenever the green-eyed monster rears its heads, I should pray for Emily?"

"Not exactly." Margie smiles. "But I think it's a good idea."

baptizing the babies

On Sunday, the boys are baptized.

I always feel like other people's baptisms are holy ground. When we baptize a baby, we all stand with the family. We promise to help them raise that child in the faith. We pray.

And I cry.

But somehow I've never felt that sense of the sacred at my own children's baptisms. I've never cried. Today is no exception.

I confess I feel a little cheated.

After church, Julianne assures me that the boys' baptism was precious and beautiful, that Luke and Ben were darling, that Jack and Jane were wholly focused and engaged as they stood next to the baptismal font with us.

I'm glad to know that because I felt disconnected, distracted.

I tried to focus on the words of Isaiah that Doug and I read.

Those who hope in the Lord will renew their strength,
* they will rise on wings like eagles,*
they will run and not grow weary,
* they will walk and not be faint.*

I've been praying these words over Ben ever since Susan shared them with me the day after he was born. I was so scared, then, that I would be reading them at his funeral. I tried to focus on those words because I promised Susan that first week of Ben's life that we would read them at his baptism, and I've been waiting all these months to make good on that promise, to have the meaning of those words—the promise of them—wash over me with joy.

And I tried to focus on the words that Renee spoke, on the water as she baptized first Ben and then Luke, on the looks on the boys' faces as the water touched their foreheads and trailed down their temples.

I tried to be present to the holiness of the moment.

But I wasn't present to the sacred. I was distracted by my juggling of the logistics of two babies, two older kids, two sets of grandparents, two godparents, and a Bible.

Pass the microphone. Pass the Bible. Pass a baby.

In all the passing, I missed the present. The wonder. The gift of standing on holy ground, surrounded by people I love.

Already, I don't remember what Renee said. Already I don't remember how the boys looked. Already I don't remember how it felt to stand in the midst of my community and be prayed for.

That is completely lame.

It is also completely okay. It really is. God saw. And God remembers. He holds those moments always, forever, and one day I will get to see my boys' baptism without the distraction of who is supposed to do what when.

I will get to see it as it truly was: God-infused, wonder-filled, joy-charged.

grace notes, april 3

Pink camellia petals scattered over green grass.

Rafts of yellow daffodils in yards, planting strips, traffic circles.

Bare branches and trunks of birch trees, bright white against a gray sky.

Birdsong.

Grape hyacinth.

Pink blossoms on trees, lining both sides of the street.

Chickadees flitting from branch to branch of the fig tree and camellia bushes outside the dining room window.

Doug "reading" Kim and Carrots from *Babybug* to all four kids and turning it into a zombie story, complete with chainsaws.

Jack's laughter.

Jane's dimples.

Baby lungs, even when they cry.

Maundy Thursday
true food

I am writing by candlelight. Everyone else is in bed. The Easter garden the kids and I made sits beside me on the table, its candles wick-black. Only the purple candle, the one we light each night at dinner, burns. I want it dark like this on this dark night. I want to feel the heaviness of this night, the love, the betrayal, the agony—or at least a little of it.

But for me, Easter began in February this year. And I am so grateful for my deliverance from darkness and fear that I do not feel the burden of Jesus' sacrifice. I feel only the joy of my deliverance. And so, on this night as we gathered in the sanctuary, I bowed my head and listened as the Scriptures were read, but I did not weep. When Renee proclaimed "the Lord's death, the Lord's saving death, until He comes again," I stood with Luke in my arms—he was nursing—and went forward, dry-eyed, to receive Communion. I felt a little self-conscious shuffling up the aisle draped in my udder cover for all and sundry to see, but Renee served me the bread and wine and then placed her hand on Luke's udder-covered head and said a blessing over him. I chewed the juice-soaked wafer and returned to my pew, Luke still in my arms. I leaned over and kissed his forehead. I smiled.

Now, sitting here beside the flickering flame of a purple candle, I see the connection: Luke was feeding on my body as I was feeding on Christ's. His is the breast on which we lean, like John at the Last Supper, from which we feed—his body, our food. What could be more perfect than to receive that living food while nursing Luke, a reminder in my own flesh of what I am doing: I am feeding on Christ. He nurses me. Nurse, nurture. I bet they have the same root. To care for, to nourish, to feed. And that is what Jesus does. He nurses me. When I come to the table, I am helpless as a baby. All I can do is open my mouth and receive the food He freely gives. His body. His blood. I eat. I drink. Like Luke.

Of course, about a minute after I sat back down in my pew, Luke spit up his food all down his front—and mine—so the image sort of falls apart.

Or maybe it doesn't. Maybe I'm yakking up all the time, too, spitting out the True Food every time I open my mouth in anger or irritation or impatience. Maybe we never outgrow the spit up stage. We just spit up in more socially acceptable ways.

I don't want to be a yakker. I want that Food to fill me, transform me. I want to eat the Bread and drink the Wine until I am so nourished by the True Food that I become what I have eaten, until I can no longer tell where I end and Christ begins, where Christ ends and I begin. Settle in, Lord. Settle deep. I want to be Your Body.

The light flickers on, a tongue of flame licking the darkness away.

Good Friday
god in the dark

These past weeks, I keep remembering at odd moments the recurring dream I had the Lent after Jack was born, the dream in which I stood— cowered, really—on a small ledge in a huge dark cave filled with water. At the far side, I could see light glimmering on the water, so I knew there was a way out. But I had no boat, no raft, no way to get from my small shelf to the far side of the cave. Unless I swam.

The waters were dark. Scary. What if they hid slimy things? Or things with sharp teeth? I cowered on the ledge, longing for the light of day, but unable to force myself into the water. Then the cave began to convulse. The ledge that I stood on shook. I shrank against the cave wall, trying to hold on, but there were no handholds, nothing to grasp. The cave lurched again, and I sprawled into the water. And swam, terrified, for the light.

I always woke up before I got to the light.

This dream always seemed to be about my fear of deep water, my fear of drowning, my fear of death. But it held within it hope: the light that glimmered on the far side of the cave, if only I could get to it.

I think I've lived that dream these past months. Only in the real-life version, I didn't have to wake up before I reached the light. Standing here, on the cusp of Easter, I've reached the far side of the cave. I'm standing in the light. And from this side, looking back over the water, light streams back into the darkness, and I see, so clearly, that what I feared—was not. The darkness that I feared—it is a deep watery abyss, yes, but at the bottom of the abyss lies a Rock, the rock who bore me through the waters of birth, of baptism, of the daily deaths and the final one, the rock who is higher than I. And that rock is a Person, just as I hoped.

Looking back across the waters, I see—so clearly—that God has indeed borne me through those waters, has been with me all along.

I see God's hand in prompting me to start taking grace notes last January, without which the darkness and the fear would have been so much darker and more frightening: looking for blessings helped me to see blessings, and the notes in my journal reminded me of God's past and present faithfulness.

I see that the words of Isaiah 9 together with the Advent sermons in December were God's words to me: Don't be afraid; I am with you.

I see God's hand in prompting me to memorize the words of Psalm 63 last fall, and, long ago, Psalm 23 and the words of that poor father with the demon-possessed son—those words that came to mind when I had no words of my own, as prayers to combat my fear.

I see that the prayers and visits and meals from my faith community were Christ's arms of love holding me.

And I see that even my ability to choose faith in the face of fear was grace, God sustaining me in the midst of my weakness. I couldn't feel my way to faith in the darkness. But God gave me the grace and the strength to choose faith anyway, to choose it in spite of my very loud fears.

I see now that in the darkness and the fear and the doubt, God was present. Even when I most feared I was alone, I was not.

I was never alone in the darkness.

I was never alone.

God was with me in the dark.

Holy Saturday
spend it all

Sun sifts down through the dining room window. The white flowers in our Easter garden catch and reflect the light. I spread my journal on the dining room table, but I don't write in it. I look out the window instead, at buds plumping up on the fig tree, at a robin sitting quietly in the branches, at a squirrel scampering across the top of the fence between our yard and Mark's. This is more or less what my world looked like this time last year. Only now I have four children instead of two.

I remember sitting in the bathroom, on the edge of the tub, as I brushed my teeth on Good Friday last year—or maybe it was the next night, or the next week—and crying. I didn't know how I was going to mother four children. Let alone mother four children and write. I still don't. But I've muddled through so far, managing to blog twice a week for the past year, even in the midst of the fear and the faith-fall. And now, thanks be to God, the darkness has receded, and life is looking hopeful again. After death—comes resurrection. That is the Christian promise, and I am so grateful to have that hope.

The robin flies away. I think maybe now that I'm sleeping more, now that I'm not expending so much energy just trying not to cry all the time, maybe I could write a bit more? Maybe even unearth my novel? It's been a year since I laid it to rest. Maybe it's time to bring it back out into the light. It seems only right, only fair—I've returned to the light. I want my beloved characters to return to the light, too.

The squirrel stops scampering and sits on its back feet, its black eyes darting, nose twitching.

Here's the thing that I keep banging into: Annie Dillard says you have to spend it all, every time. This morning I thought, I have to break the bottle, like Mary did when she poured nard on Jesus' feet. No holding back. Give it all.

And I don't. I hold back, out of fear—that I'll need that bit later, or that it will come across wrong, or that it will lead to failure.

The squirrel leaps from the fence into the fig tree. *Or success.* The fig branches bounce as the squirrel bounds from one to another and out of my sight.

I am afraid of success? It's not like I'm in any danger of it, if by "success" one means publication of multiple books and something approaching a living wage. But I still fear it—even as I feel jealous of Emily right now. Margie said my envy could teach me something, and I think it's trying to shout past my fear. It's yelling that it's time to quit fixating on my failure and break the bottle.

Jean Rhys once told an interviewer, "All of writing is a huge lake. There are great rivers that feed the lake, like Dostoevsky and Tolstoy. and there are mere trickles, like Jean Rhys. All that matters is feeding the lake. I don't matter. The lake matters. You must keep feeding the lake."

I think my envy is shouting that it's time to get over myself and feed the lake. It's time to stop standing on the shore and enter the wide river of God's mercy, to become one of the drops in that stream rushing down to the lake. The vastness of that scares me. Just like in my dream—all that water. The responsibility scares me. The possibilities scare me—I could be swept away.

But haven't I already been swept away? Isn't that what this whole last year has done—swept away my old self, forcing me to lean harder on Jesus, so I don't drown? Maybe the sweeping away, scary as it is, is a grace because it keeps me gasping for Jesus, clinging to Him, swimming in His strength.

Spend it all.

Spending it all may not look like success. It sure didn't for Jesus— laid in the earth after His humiliating crucifixion. Spending it all may look like failure, like those 14 boxes of books in my basement. But I'm starting to see that my faithfulness in feeding the lake matters more than how much bigger the lake gets because of my faithfulness.

Outside the window, nothing stirs, except the branches of the fig tree in the slightest of breezes. I open the window a crack, to feel the air myself. On the other side of the screen, a bee lands on a camellia blossom.

Feed the lake. Spend it all. Again and again and again. That is what God asks.

The rest is not my business.

Easter
an epilogue of sorts
(april)

When the Lord restored the fortunes of Zion,
  we were like those who dream.
Then our mouth was filled with laughter,
  and our tongues with shouts of joy;
then they said among the nations,
  "The Lord has done great things for them."
The Lord has done great things for us;
  we are glad.

—Psalm 126

glory at the gas pump

We gather at Mosaic Coffee House, these six women and I, to discuss
Those Who See, Emily Barrett's bestseller that I love and that makes me
despair of ever being a real writer, by which I mean, a writer like she is.

When Tiffany suggested this as our April read, I had to laugh. I
mean, *of course* this is the book we would be reading and discussing
as I work through my envy issues with its author. But I have heeded
Margie's advice, and I use my jealousy as a call to pray for Emily—that
God would bless the work of her hands and surround her with his love
as with a shield as she walks this new road—so that my envious heart
doesn't get the best of me.

I'm not the only one feeling envious. At one point, Laura says, "Am I
the only one who thought, 'Oh come on. You live in rural Montana for
heaven's sake, with your awesome husband and your beautiful children
and your sixteen chickens and your goats and your bees. How hard can
life be?' I mean, I know she's had a hard life. I get that she struggles. But
sometimes it just felt really idyllic, and I'm having a hard time taking
what she says about beauty and goodness and God and applying it to
my life in the middle of the city."

Laura doesn't say, *to my life with my husband who is not the person I
thought he was.* She doesn't say, *my life with my marriage that is falling
apart, with my kids who are caught in the middle of a mess they didn't
make.* But she could have. I can only imagine how reading about
Emily's supportive husband must feel like so much salt in the cracks of
her own failing marriage.

No one speaks for a moment, so I say, "The other day, I was at Costco, the one up at Aurora Village." They know how much I hate Costco, how I loathe big box stores of any stripe. "I was waiting in the gas line, and everywhere I looked there were cars and buses and big windowless buildings. You know how it is—strip mall hell up there."

They laugh.

"So I'm standing there, pumping gas into the minivan, and it smells like gasoline, and it's noisy with all the cars and buses driving around the parking lot and on that street up above the gas station, and there was *nothing* beautiful to look at. Nothing. Just the cars and the buildings and the buses, and I thought the exact same thing as you, Laura. I thought, it must be easy to see God when you live in the country surrounded by natural beauty. But then I remembered something Ruth Haley Barton said in one of her books, about how growing close to God can happen in the midst of the life we have; we just have to want it badly enough to do something about it.

"So I looked around, and I thought, *Okay, God, what's one thing I can find around here to focus on that's beautiful?* And I looked up, and away to the right, beyond the power lines, was a glimpse of blue sky framed by trees—they had that soft green fuzz of new spring growth still on them—and I thought, *That's it. I can focus on that.* And I did. I stood there, and I looked at the sky and the trees and ignored the power lines, and I thanked God for that small slice of beauty."

Elaine says, "Yes! Kimberlee, yes! That's exactly it! That's what this whole book is all about—about finding the beauty, the grace, the goodness right where we are. And you did it." She grins at me. "You found glory at the gas pump."

I laugh. We all laugh.

The conversation swirls on. Laughter. Thoughtfulness. The beautiful faces of these women who have walked—are walking—a hard road with me, with Tiffany, with Laura.

But I am still thinking about Elaine's words. *Yes. Yes, I did: I found glory at the gas pump.* I found glory everywhere this past year. I had to look for it. But Jesus says, "Seek and you will find." And He is right: I sought, and I found.

I think whenever I—whenever anyone—finds goodness and grace, that's glory. And when we find goodness and grace in hard and hurting places, that's glory squared: because in those hard and hurting places, it's so clear that we are not the manufacturers of the grace and goodness. We just receive it as the gift it is. Michaela's healing, Ben's healing, Lynne's healing, my healing.

And whenever we come alongside others in their weakness and pain, that's glory. As Tiffany walked the long, hard road of chemo with Michaela, we bore what little of her pain we could. These women, and my larger church community, walked the hard road of postpartum depression with me and bore my pain as much as they could. And we will walk alongside Laura as her marriage deteriorates, bearing as much of her pain as we can. That is the way of Jesus, the way of the cross, the way of costly love.

The way of glory.

So I think maybe I didn't just find glory this year. I think maybe glory found me, too, through these women sitting here, and through Doug and my children and the people at my church and every friend or stranger who offered words of comfort or just a Kleenex so I could blow my nose and wipe my weepy eyes.

Laughter ripples around the table, and I remember what I told Margie right around this time last year—Anne Lamott's line, "laughter is carbonated holiness." Now I would add that it's also a triumph over the darkness, a form of praise. I might even say it's glory.

As I look at these women—these beloved friends—at their smiling, laughing faces, joy swells in my chest, in that place where the anxiety and fear used to sit like boulders, and I can't keep it down. It rises right up, like the Psalmist's evening incense. It fills my mouth and opens my lips, and I laugh, too.

S. D. G.

author's note

For reasons both personal and literary, I have changed the names of some of the people mentioned in the book, created composites of some of the minor characters (smushing two or more of my real-life friends together into one character), and rearranged some (minor) events.

thanks, thanks, and ever thanks

So many people contributed to my well-being both during the course of events that this book portrays and during its writing that all the pages of all the books in all the world probably couldn't do justice to their kindness and generosity to me and my family. Still, here's a stab at saying my most heartfelt *thank you*.

The people of Bethany Presbyterian Church—many of whom I didn't (and still don't) know—made meals for our family for six months. The gift of that food week after week saved me more anxiety than even I know. My church family also holds me in so many ways—carrying my faith when I can't, praying for and with me and my kids, singing over me as I weep, yet again, through the worship songs. These brothers and sisters are the salt of the earth, the light shining on a hill, and I am so glad to call them family.

Margie VanDuzer regularly speaks wisdom into my confusion, helps me pay attention to where God is in my life, and gives me space to just be.

Susan Forshey, soul-sister and dearest of friends, exhorts, encourages, and, when needed, remonstrates. I am so grateful for her steadfast companionship on this journey of life and faith.

Tiffany Werner prayed for me and cried with me. Her friendship as we walked our separate hard roads together made my hard road less hard, for which I am forever grateful. I also thank her daughters Madeline and Michaela for graciously allowing me to share the parts of their story that intersected with mine.

The women of my book group—Tonia Davidson, Cindy Hagen, Kathy Keith, Cynthia McConnelee-Smith, Janice Waszak, and Tiffany Werner—suggest great books to read and discuss. Without them, my literary life would be infinitely poorer. I'm also deeply grateful that they read a late draft of this book and provided me with invaluable critique and much-needed encouragement.

Mick Silva, my editor, read this book in draft form and was able to see in it what I wanted it to be rather than what it was. His words of encouragement, repeated readings of various drafts, and invaluable editorial input made this book what it is, and I am so thankful.

Melody Fosmore, my Tuesday angel, came every week for six months to keep me company, make meals, mop my floors, and help me bathe my babies. I'm not sure how I would have survived those first six months postpartum without her.

John and Peggy Ireton, my amazing in-laws, drove three hours every week for almost two years to hang out with my kids and help me stay sane.

Lynne Baab, Cindy Hagen, Amy Larson, Michelle Layton, Dianne Ross, Julia Sensenbrenner, Janice Waszak, and Karen Wooten incarnated Jesus to me through the meals they made me, the timely words they spoke to my soul, the childcare they freely offered, and most especially their friendship.

Lori Reimann Garretson organized meals and household help for our family for almost five months. Words can't express my gratitude. Lori also proofread the manuscript of this book, catching errors I'd missed, even after dozens of readings.

My mother spent—gave up, really—two months of her life to be with me after the twins were born. I can't imagine how difficult it must have been for her to be away from home with a daughter who often took for granted the gift of her help, presence, and care.

My parents, Chris and Carol Conway, have encouraged my writing since I was old enough to hold a pencil. They published my first book when I was six and have always been genuinely proud of me, for which I am both amazed and thankful.

My sister, Jen Barrow, helps me laugh at myself—or at her. In the two weeks (of summer vacation!) that she spent with me after the twins were born, she embarked on the nasty task of clearing out all of the junk in my house, including four years of crap that had accumulated in my catch-all basement. My house never looked so good…and likely never will again.

My children, Jack, Jane, Luke, and Ben, have stretched me in ways I never could have imagined. I am so grateful to be their mother and learn from them how to be a better parent, a better person. I am also grateful for their daily grace and forgiveness as I lurch along this path of raising them.

And finally, though never least, my husband Doug is my corner when I need someplace safe to cry or hide, believes in me and my writing (this, despite those boxes of books in the basement that would make a lesser man think otherwise), keeps me from taking myself too seriously, and never tires of cheering me on. The man deserves a Medal of Honor, but he'll have to settle for an inscribed copy of this book.

And of course, to the triune God, Father, Son, and Holy Spirit, be all thanks and praise and glory and honor and power, now and forever.

notes

Advent: the baby cometh

Epigram: George MacDonald, *Diary of an Old Soul* (Minneapolis: Augsburg, 1994), July 15.

Triduum: the end of life as I know it

Epigram: Anne Lamott, *Operating Instructions: A Journal of My Son's First Year* (New York: Fawcett Columbine, 1993), p. 113.

page 20: "A new commandment…" John 13:34 NRSV

Easter: a season of laughter

Epigram: *Diary of an Old Soul*, July 9.

Ordinary Time: girth

Epigram: Luke 2:5 KJV

page 65: "It is only with the heart…" Antoine de Saint-Exupery, trans. Katherine Woods, *The Little Prince* (San Diego: Harcourt Brace and Company, 1943), p. 73.

Ordinary Time: birth

Epigram: Matthew 11:28, ESV

page 84: "Those who hope…" Isaiah 40:31 NIV. Also on pages 170 and 237.

page 98: "a Beautiful South song…" Paul Heaton and Dave Rotheray, "36D," *0898 Beautiful South*. Go! Discs, 1992.

Ordinary Time: zombies

Epigram: *Diary of an Old Soul*, September 12.

Ordinary Time: jackals

Epigram: Psalm 63:8-10 from *Book of Common Worship: Daily Prayer* (Louisville: Westminster John Knox Press, 1993).

Advent: the darkness deepens

Epigram: Psalm 55:4 ESV; *Diary of an Old Soul*, November 2.

page 164: "The people who walked…" Isaiah 9:2 NRSV

page 177: "Surely you and I…" Amy Grant, Chris Eaton, Robert Marshall, "Emmanuel, God With Us," *Home for Christmas*. Sparrow Records, 1992.

Christmas: hard to believe

Epigram: Mark 5:36 NRSV

page 188: "Then Jesus said…" John 8:31-32 NRSV

page 194: "In the Lord I'll be ever thankful…" Jacques Berthier / Taizé, *In the Lord I'll Be Ever Thankful*, Ateliers et Presses de Taizé, France, 1986, 1991.

Epiphany: the color of hope

Epigram: *Diary of an Old Soul*, July 28.

Lent: the light lengthens

Epigram: Psalm 30:1-3 NIV

page 229: "A soft answer…" Proverbs 15:1 ESV

page 245: "Jean Rhys once told an interviewer…" qtd. in Madeleine L'Engle, *Walking on Water: Reflections on Faith & Art* (Wheaton, Illinois: Harold Shaw Publishers, 1980), p. 23

Easter: an epilogue of sorts

Epigram: Psalm 126:1-3 ESV

CPSIA information can be obtained at www.ICGtesting.com
Printed in the USA
LVOW05s2249220714

395593LV00004B/316/P